NAKED UNDER OUR CLOTHES

ED LOVER AND DOCTOR DRÉ

UNZIPPED, UNCUT, AND TOTALLY UNPLUGGED

A FIRESIDE BOOK / PUBLISHED BY SIMON & SCHUSTER / New York London Toronto Sydney Tokyo Singapore

FIRESIDE
Rockefeller Center
1230 Avenue of the Americas
New York, NY 10020

FIRESIDE and colophon are registered trademarks
of Simon & Schuster Inc.

Illustrations by Lynwood Bernard Peele

Manufactured in the United States of America

1   3   5   7   9   10   8   6   4   2

Library of Congress Cataloging-in-Publication Data
available upon request.

ISBN 0-684-82368-3

"Unplugged" is a trademark of MTV Networks, a division of Viacom
International, Inc. Its use herein is with the permission of MTV Networks.

ACKNOWLEDGMENTS

We would like to acknowledge the following people. For all of their hard work and patience in helping us to put this book together, we say thanks:

To Charlie Stettler: For being a friend, leader, father, teacher, salesman, and most of all babysitter! We say thank you and we love you dearly, forever.

To Lynda West: For sticking with us and explaining things in good ol' plain English whenever Charlie confused us and for your writing and designing and literary skills, we love you too. VIVA MOMMA THE MAC!!!

To the whole support unit: to Kim Taylor for the great makeup jobs; to Carl Posey for the dynamite flicks; to our homeboys for the inspiration; and to the whole staff at Simon and Schuster. Thanks a million.

And last but certainly not least, to the woman who put her life and career on hold to make sure this tome came out right: DAWN DANIELS, writer, editor, babysitter, and most of all *friend*. Dawn, we cannot thank you enough for all that you've done and sacrificed for this project. You've truly gone well beyond the duties of an editor. You are one beautiful, classy lady, and we have been truly blessed to have had the chance to work with someone like you. Without you, this book truly would have never been done. THANK YOU, THANK YOU, THANK YOU!!!! WE LOVE YOU!!!!

DEDICATION

I would like to dedicate this book to James E. Roberts Sr. I'm still missin' ya!

—Ed Lover

I would like to dedicate this book to a gentleman who showed me what friendship and raw courage were all about throughout our friendship until his untimely death in September 1995. Hip-hop, the rap music industry, and most of all his family and friends will miss him. Therefore, I would like to dedicate this book to the life and memory of Dave "Funken" Klein.

—Doctor Dre

CONTENTS

Hobnobbing with the Goober Smoochers   89

IS IT IN THERE?

 "**INTRODUCTION**" is such a boring way to get into a book. Most people don't even read

the damn thing, so we thought we'd rename it. I'm sure Dr. Ruth would like to begin her books with "Is it

in there?" rather than a boring section titled "Introduction." Right, Ed.  Sure, Dre. I'd like to know

that everything I want to know about is in there. If it isn't in the book, why did I spend $11 on the damn

thing? I think we have, yet again, changed the way people look at the world. Good move, partner.

At this point we're sure you're saying to yourselves, "What do two Black guys from New York have to say

about life?" A lot, dammit! What Ed's trying to say is that we have had a lot of things happen to us and we have stories to tell. Whow, whow, whow—wait a minute there, Dre. We not only have

a lot to put in your ears, we give it to you straight. No beatin' around the bush, no pussy-footin' around,

no sissy lollygaggin' . . . Anyway, Ed and I want to let you know that we've seen a lot of situations,

experienced things that I would've never dreamed of, and now we want to pass some of the things we've

learned on to you folks. Our basic philosophy in life is simple: We believe that no matter how bad things

seem, you can always find humor in the realness. Dre, tell them the real story. If you get fucked

out the game, you can always laugh your ass right back in. It's just that simple. If you didn't know, now you

know! We're not into cryin' like little babies. We're making the bad look good, the ugly beautiful, the

bizarre reality, the rich poor, the old young . . . Ed gets lost in his thoughts sometimes, but he means

well. We want to let everyone know that it can all be dynamite if you look at things from different angles.

There have been things that were difficult for us to stomach, but . . . Dre, there's nothing too difficult for you to stomach! Forget the "looking at the angle" stuff. Know what you're gettin' your ass into and you'll be on point. Just so you know where we're comin' from, we're gonna tell you a little bit about where we came from, how we were raised, and the dysfunctional things that shaped me and Ed's philosophy about life. Of course we're gonna let you know about all the things that happened along the way and how that makes us the great philosophers we are today. So sit back on the couch with a bowl of popcorn and . . . You know that was Dre 'cause don't nobody read a book with a bowl of popcorn. Keep it real, Dre, like I know your Pops told you. Take this book to the bathroom with you. You know, when you have to make a deposit, the big #2, the El Dumpo. Sit back, strain, relax between plops, and read. I'm tellin' you, this book is better than any laxative Mom Dukes ever gave you. You'll find yourselves in the bathroom with us even when you don't have to make a deposit. You'll just sit on the toilet and flush as you read. I know when I'm reading a good book, a flush or two just makes it real dynamite!

 Ed, you know they can read this book anywhere. And you're right for a change, Ed. My father did say you always have some free time to read. No excuses. And when all else fails, you always have a few quiet minutes to sit down in the bathroom. I told you, Dre! Don't hold back on our friends 'cause we're all naked under our clothes. We can't hide shit! I'm sure you know about that because you've got a lot more to hide than most of us. If you didn't know, now you know. Okay, Ed, enough said. I think I'll speak for both of us in that case when I say: Just read the damn book!

"WE'VE ONLY JUST BEGUN..."

—The Carpenters

THURSDAY, August 17, 1995, was the first day of the rest of our lives. It was the last day of *Yo! MTV Raps*. Dre, Ed, and Ted sat down and programmed the most powerful show that rap music had ever seen in its whole fuckin' entire life and now it's over, or as the rap group Channel Live put it, reprogrammed. On the last show we got the support of the true celebs like Chuck D, KRS-One, Salt-n-Pepa, Method Man, Redman, Chubb Rock, Flavor Flav,

Rakim, MC Lyte, Special Ed, Lost Boys, MC Serch, and a lot of other rappers.

During *Yo! MTV Raps*'s high point we were the most-watched show on the channel. Plain and simple.

Understand, when Dre and I went into MTV, Ted Demme and Peter Dougherty were the only two muthafuckers that gave a fuck about Ed Lover and Doctor Dre. We auditioned separately, but

Ted put us together. Ted had the foresight to say, "They're both good, but if I put them together they'd be great." And when we walked in there and did our thing nobody gave a flying fuck. Understand that show was done under budget, that show was done for pennies in comparison to some of the other shows. We used to take stuff from other people's sets and improvise to use it to make the *Yo!* set work. Boy, those were the days!

We interviewed celebrities of all magnitudes. If Ed went to a club and Bobby Brown was there and he slapped that, "Yo Bobby! We're shooting *Yo!* tomorrow," Bobby would show up. So now all the red tape that we would normally have to go through wasn't necessary. Bobby shows up on *Yo!*, then the viewers go crazy and say to their friends, "Yo! Bobby Brown's on *Yo! MTV Raps!*" They watched *Yo!* They watched the channel because of *Yo!*

The artists watched the show and then they wanted to be on *Yo!* so when you saw 'em they would come up to us and say, "When am I going to be on your show? When you gonna let me be on *Yo!?*" For instance, like the time I first met Denzel Washington, he turned around and said, "Damn, Ed, you look taller than that on television." I'm stunned, so I say, "You watch *Yo! MTV Raps*??!" Denzel goes, "Yeah, I watch it with my kids all the time." Bill Cosby called Ed 'cause his daughter told him to watch *Yo!* and he checked it out. So it wasn't like celebrities had to go through the regular channels to get on the show, and because of that, our fellow employees said we were stepping on people's toes. Whoever was in charge of talent, artist relations would try to book these people for different shows on MTV, and the artists or celebrities didn't want to do that. They wanted to do *Yo! MTV Raps*.

The funniest shit we can remember was an interview with Mike Tyson just before Mike was sent to prison. We're filming *Yo! MTV Raps* and Mike says, "Let's go over to the golf course, we're gonna shoot it over there." Because they couldn't find the key to unlock the gate, Mike hops the fence. Ted hops the fence. I hop the fence. Don King and Dre are left standing there looking at the fence. So Dre's like, "You know, Don, if you can do it I can do it." Don says the hell with it and he decided to wait there until we came back with the key. Then all of a sudden I hear, "Come on, Dre." Dre looks at the fence then looks at me looking at the fence. So he figured it was time to attempt to make this fence. So he valiantly climbed on top of this fence and then you hear "Urnnnn." I go, "Ah hell, that's it. Now we've got to pay for a fence too." We shot a couple of segments with Dre sitting on top of the fence. Then Mike's going, "He broke my fuckin' fence. Don, we need to work Doctor Dre out. Get off my fuckin' fence. Don, can we work Dre?

Dre: "Hey Mike, couldn't you afford a sturdier fence?"

Mike: "I'll show you a sturdier fence!" Pow!

We'll have him skinny. He'll live with me. He'll run with me." Mike was serious about that, too.

THAT'S how it all began. We would take videos that would normally get only regional exposure and give them national and international play. We played what we wanted to play when we wanted to play it. You know how much power that is, when 50 million people are looking at you? When we played N.W.A, N.W.A wasn't anywhere near where they are today. Before we played their videos there were 150,000 records sold. After we played them they sold 2 million copies in three fuckin' months. Do you know what kinda power that is?—to say, "All right, I'm playing this. No, fuck this Hammer video, I'm not playing it!" **We didn't just play rap videos.** We were the first ones that started playing funk, reggae, and alternative Black records. We played anything that fit what we felt made the show work. We played anything that was hip, young, and especially Black.

There were a lot of times when we would be out during the heyday of *Yo! MTV Raps* and got video promoters from certain record companies that would offer us money to play their videos, because they knew we had the power to play whatever we wanted to play. They knew that we could play one video four times in a week and that meant record sales and that made the promoters look like they knew what they were doing. Before *Yo! MTV Raps* there was nobody that was hitting 50 million homes every day with videos. There was no outlet for it. So when Dre and I started programming along with Ted, we played what we wanted and what we thought was good. We would do a whole day of L. L. Cool J videos—ten L. L. Cool J videos in a row. You know what that meant for L. L.'s record sales? We would do ten of Kool Moe Dee's joints, and we had Big Daddy Kane Day—all Big Daddy Kane videos for the entire show!

After a couple of years of being one of the **#1-rated shows on MTV,** things started to change. Time slots were switched and we were "relieved" of our programming responsibilities. Then the excuses started pouring in. "Oh, they don't show up no more." What that had to do with was we had power and they saw that power every Spring Break. The concept for Spring Break was started right on the set of *Yo! MTV Raps*. We held a beach bikini babe contest one season and after we had several beautiful bikini-clad women walk across the set of *Yo! MTV Raps,* the concept for Spring Break began.

Everybody went crazy for us, from the first one we went down to, to the last one we attended. The fact that when we went to Spring Break and they did a *Yo! MTV Raps* live, and hundreds of Black people came from Daytona and all neighboring Black colleges, said a lot. Of course with so many young people converging on one beach, shit got rowdy. Do you know who were the only ones that could

Spring Break. Me surrounded by half-naked people.

stand up and calm 'em down! Ed and Dre. Dre and Ed. That was it. Ed and Dre were the only ones that could stand up and say, "Yo chill out!" And everyone calmed down.

When MTV would go down for Spring Break what was startin' to happen is the fusion of every-body—Black, white, Latino, Asian, you name it—comin' at the same time. We would go down and then

Doctor Dre   Ed Lover

the week after our Spring Break the Black Spring Break would happen. We knew that. The Black college organizations would call us to go back down and host their main event without *Yo! MTV Raps.* They said, You can bring the MTV cameras if you want. So we would go all right, and you know what? We brought MTV with us anyway. They never felt like MTV was coming for their Spring Break. No, it was the other way around: Ed and Dre were coming and we just happened to bring the *Yo! MTV Raps* crew with us. We walked around, did a couple of episodes, but that wasn't the main attraction, because Black college kids wanted us there more than MTV.

BEFORE *Yo! MTV Raps* started, there was no music under the video jock segments. None. None. It was plain you and the background. Downtown Julie Brown did her thing, cut, and go to the video. Before *Yo! MTV Raps,* there was no dialogue between different VJs and stuff like that, or skits. They sent a memo to us saying, "You guys are going too long. Gotta make the segments shorter, gotta make it shorter." The show we created was a show inside a channel that gave an entertainment value to the programming.

We changed the face of MTV!

WITH seven years on *Yo! MTV Raps,* television specials, movies, records, management companies, record labels, clothing lines, and one of New York's top-rated radio shows under our belts, so many people think we were friends since day one. A lot of people make the mistake of thinking we were best friends since we were in diapers or we went to school together or we're Siamese twins joined at the hip. Imagine that: Ed connected to Dre's hip. I'd get lost in the sauce!

The point is Ed and I didn't meet each other until we were in our twenties. We never laid eyes on each other before that. But we can say one thing: We grew up in very similar neighborhoods and had colorful childhoods.

Me and Dre definitely got our own vibe. That's what makes it work. I met Dre at the audition for *Yo! MTV Raps.* The thing that I remember about Dre was that he was fat. I was like, Damn, that's a big motherfucker. That's the first thing I remember about Dre.

The first thing I remember about Ed was that asshole's got a big fuckin' mouth and he's too goddamn rude!

I came there and Dre was there for the same reason I was. I remember him coming up to me and saying, "Yo, what's up? I'm Doctor Dre," like I was supposed to know who the fuck he was. So I was like, "Yeah, so what? My name is Ed. How ya doing?" He went over to see Ted and then he came back over and I asked him was he there for the audition for *Yo! MTV Raps?*

I was like "Yeah." Then Ted brought us over at the same time and we taped stuff together. That was vision to place Ed and myself together, and it didn't matter to me because I was excited to work.

Charlie came into the picture a couple of years after we started *Yo! MTV Raps*. Dre and I still didn't have a manager, then Charlie was the only one that really cared about us. We were supposed to be down with Russell, but he hardly got us any work and never did much of anything for us.

Ed, let's save the rest of the MTV thing for them later. How about we tell them a little about our childhoods for now.

Okay, Dre. We're gonna highlight some of these special, tearjerking, heart-tuggin', emotional, joyful . . .

Ed, shut up and let's tell them how things were!

TINY TOTS

MISTY watercolor memories of the way Ed was:

My earliest memories of childhood revolve around the toilet. Boy, did I love to flush the toilet. My mother can and will concur, at the tender age of eleven months I would climb out of my crib, crawl backwards down two whole flights of stairs, and go flush the toilet. And let me tell you, we had one beautiful toilet. Big and shiny white porcelain with the box separated from the bowl. You had to yank the chain in order to flush it and I became a pro at it. I would stand there mesmerized watching the water go around and around. *Whoosh!* I would yank the chain. *Whoosh!* There she goes again. *Whoosh!* Over and over until my mother came to get me out. The next day I would sneak out and do it all over again.

I can also remember climbing out of my crib to sneak down the stairs, through the basement of the brownstone. This way I could go out the basement door, which was always unlocked, and sit on the stoop in front of the house. I would just sit out there in my little cloth diaper and sleeveless white T-shirt in the summertime, sucking my thumb and saying hello to whoever walked by. My mother says the landlady, Mrs. Jones, used to call to her, "Mrs. Roberts, your baby's outside again!" That's the only way she would know I was gone. I never went off the stoop, I just stayed on that stoop and spoke to all the people who passed my way. I guess that's where I get my gift of gab from. I could walk and talk clearly at eleven months. **Once I began to talk, I never shut up** even if it got me into trouble, which it often has.

We can all see where Ed picked up his anal-retentive tendencies and his oral fixations. My baby stories aren't as dysfunctional, but definitely interesting.

It all started back when, when I was only knee high to a, a, a, anyway . . .

Ever since I can remember, **I walked around the house naked as the day I was born,** naked as a jaybird. Feelin' very comfortable with the skin I'm in. Why I don't know. It's probably some kind of a ritual thing.

The day I realized it wasn't normal to walk around naked I was just five years old. My mom was having a Tupperware party and was busy entertaining her guests. Of course, at five years old you want to be where all the good food and action was at, so my brother and I were in the kitchen picking at the plates until we were shooed away. You must know my brother always played mean tricks on me, since I was the youngest, and this day was no exception. You see, after all the picking and sipping we were doing in the kitchen I had to go to the bathroom. My first natural instinct was to go to my mother and ask her to help me. I don't know if you remember way back when, but in those days mothers put childproof outfits on kids. My mother was no exception. She used to put these Little Lord Fauntleroy outfits on me that buttoned in the back so I couldn't take them off any time or any place, because I was known to do that in class. The teacher had to call my mother every other day and tell her that I stripped for the class. Anyway, I tugged on my mother's dress and said, "Mommy, I have to go to the baffroom." When you're in the middle of selling Miss Seola Tupperware and trying to entertain a group full of women, your attention span is a little short, so my mother said, "Dre, get out of my face. You see I have company. Go get your brother Fred to help you." I go to Fred and say, "Fred, I got to go to the baffroom! I gotta go to the baffroom!"

Fred's laughing at me and saying, "I'm not taking you." "Mom! I gotta go to the baffroom!!!!" My mother comes in the kitchen with that mother look on her face and tells Fred in a low, hushed voice, "Fred, you better take that boy to the bathroom right now or else you won't be able to sit down for a month." Well, you know Fred begrudgingly rushed me to the bathroom, but he also had revenge on his mind. When I came out of the bathroom, I had no clothes on and Fred said, "Dre, Mommy wants you. She has something for you in the living room." I love being naked, so I don't care. I just walk happily in the living room with a big grin on my face, thinking that I'm gonna get something. I got something all right, but it wasn't hardly what I ex-

Lord Fauntleroy goes to Sunday school.

pected. I'm naked except for my socks and shoes walking into a room full of talking Black women—need I say more? The room went quiet and my mother turned around and put her hands over her face.

Well, Fred and I stood in the backyard for the rest of the afternoon because we were unable to sit for a couple of hours. At least I know how to break up a good Tupperware party.

THE SHERIFF
AND THE WARDEN

BOY, we we're some cute babies there, Dre. We were movers and shakers in our diapers.

Yeah, Ed, but some of us moved and shook just a little too much. I must say that my moving and shaking was put in line for me by the Sheriff and the Warden.

I know exactly what you mean, Dre. Good old Mom and Dad. Mom was the Sheriff because she set down the laws and carried out the punishment. Dad was the Warden 'cause he made sure you listened to the Sheriff and put you in line if necessary.

I remember my first experience when my mom put on that Sheriff's hat and put law down into effect just like it was yesterday, Ed. How about you?

Dre, I feared my mom—a.k.a. Big Vi the Sheriff—more than my father. I could get out of an ass whippin' with my father because he was always tired from working two jobs. But my mother was never too tired to whip some ass.

I know what you mean, Ed, but it was sort of the other way around for me. I used to be in fear of my father because he worked too many jobs. So for him to take time off from work to deal with a problem I created became a money thing. That was extra trouble because that meant that something wasn't going to get paid. Boy, oh boy, not only did you get a whippin' from Mrs. Sheriff Brown, but you

Li'l Dre: dancin' machine.

Li'l Ed: most wanted by the Sheriff.

got a lecture from Mr. Brown the Warden, and you know how those lectures were.

The worst experience I had with the Sheriff and the Warden, Dre, was when I made the Sheriff cry. The worst thing my mom could do to me is cry. I'd rather get an ass whippin' or be put on punishment than see my mom cry. Once I played hooky for three days, and I got torn up. Even worse than getting torn up was having my mother sit there and cry right in front of me. Dre, man, there was nothing I could do to make her stop crying. It affected me worse than her hitting me. You're a low piece of shit if you make your mother cry. My father looked at me with disdain and disgust, like, Get out of my face, you're a piece of crap. My father didn't speak to me for three days because I made my mother cry. He sent me messages through my brothers. That hurt me worst than any whippin' they could ever give me.

Damn, Ed, you really messed up that time. I remember that old saying, The walls have ears, and boy was it true! There were Sheriffs and Wardens all over the place when I was little. If you messed up down the block not only would your Sheriff tear you up, but the Sheriff who caught you would tear you up too.

Dre, when I went down the street and I messed up, Miss Ernestine down the street would beat my ass. Then she'd send

Sheriff and Warden Roberts.

us home to Mrs. Roberts' and we'd get another ass whippin' and when you whipped your kid's ass, it wasn't none of that, "I'm gonna call BCW because it's abuse." That's not abuse. My father would look at me and say, "Boy, I made you, I'll kill you and make another one that looks just like you." Since my father worked two jobs, he used to say, "Boy, I'd beat your ass if I wasn't so sleepy right now. 'Cause you stupid." I thought my name was Stupid for a while. Mom and Dad did not play. All they asked us to do was our chores and bring home good grades. But of course I didn't listen. I had to be the class clown. But the values they instilled in us are wonderful. They used to say things to me like "A hard head makes a sore behind. Don't let the doorknob hit ya where the Good Lord split ya." That came directly from my mother and father.

Sheriff and Warden Brown.

I've heard all those good ol' sayings, Ed, but there was one that always baffled me. Whenever I got upset about not being able to do or have something, my father would say "tough titties," and I had to think about it. "Tough titties" made me laugh for a long time after I realized what it was.

Dre, I still don't know what "tough titties" are. Tell me.

You know, Ed, "tough titties"—titties that are tough without the milk.

Class clown.

Okay, Dre, whatever you say. Besides everything that I can remember, I would say the lessons they taught were the most memorable things. One thing I can say, they weren't always obvious. When I was young my father would call me from the window, stop me from playing freeze tag, and say, "Num Num, come turn the channel for me and fix the antenna." First of all, you can imagine how embarrassing it was for your dad to yell "Num Num" out the window for the whole neighborhood to hear? What kind of shit was that? I'm thinking to myself, The energy that he spent to open the window and call me, he could have did it. But the point is respect, and I do the same thing to my daughter Tiffany.

I remember all those lessons and then some, and I must say my pop was an incredible man. I miss him just as much as I know you miss your dad, Ed.

I know, Dre, but our dads can look at us and laugh now because being the class clown is what he used to tear my behind up for and now it's what helps support our families.

Thank you, James Edwin Roberts Sr. and Alfred James Brown Sr.

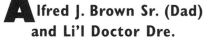 **lfred J. Brown Sr. (Dad) and Li'l Doctor Dre.**

ED'S GANG

WE all had the gang we grew up with. Curt was my best friend when I moved on the block in Queens. Curt was my road dawg. We played together all the time. We were like two peas in a pod. We did everything together, like eating potato chips and reading comic books on top of the garage when were weren't supposed to be on top of the garage. We used to hit my sister in the back of the head with mud balls. We also took her Barbie doll and make her have simulated sex with G.I. Joe. Boy, was it hard to make them two have sex, since they really didn't have anything down there to work with.

I remember my dad used to sleep so hard you'd think he was drunk. We used to always ask him for money when he was asleep. We'd be like, "Dad, can I have some money?" and he'd be like, "No!" He always told me no. So we used to send Sonya to ask for ice cream money because she's the only girl and the youngest. Most of the time he said yes and we had ice cream money. Sonya could get away with more than we could because she's the baby girl.

Me and Curt would try anything. Absolutely anything that we thought might be true. One time we heard if you eat cat food, it will make you run faster. So we tried it and we were like, "Damn! I can run faster." That was until we got sick and threw up all over the place. We put lighter fluid on cats' tails and lighted them up to make them run faster. Me and Curt also heard that cats always land on their feet. So Curt and I dragged the cat up to Curt's attic to throw it out the window. I remember just before we were going to throw the cat out of Curt's attic window, his parents caught us. They were like, "What are you doing with that cat?" The first thing we said was "Nothin'." That's a kid's favorite line when they're asked "What are you doing?" The funny thing about it was that it was Curt's family cat and we were going to toss it out of the window just to see if it would land on its feet.

We were stupid little kids who didn't have any sense sometimes and thought we were having fun. I

Me and Curt one summer
(Curt was takin' the picture).

would never let my daughter, or any child for that matter, do anything stupid like the things we did back then. We have to teach our children respect for nature and other creatures, and now when I look back at those days, I regret some of the things we did— especially to Curt's cat. I don't regret everything. We had a good childhood. We played softball, football, soccer, skelly, dodgeball, red light green light, 1-2-3, freeze tag, and so on. Back then, kids had more of a chance to be kids than they do today.

When we were young there was a guy who lived around the way, and his name was Phil. His nickname was Faggot Phil because he played with the girls. He talked like a girl, he played with girlie dolls, and he jumped double Dutch. If there was a name describing something you did or what you were, it stuck with you. For a long time, Curt was known as Cry Baby Curt because whenever Curt would get in a fight or argued with someone, he would cry. So we called him Cry Baby Curt for years.

Curt and I are together to this day. Through thick and thin. We never disrespect each other and if we get into a beef we settle it like we did back when we were kids. Argue it out 'til the end. Right, Cry Baby Curt?

Curt and I are together to this day. He's no longer known as Cry Baby Curt, but now he's Curt Flirt. Yeah, that's right! He has his own morning show on Hot 97, but more about that later.

SPIN THE BOTTLE

Dre, I was spinning the ol' bottle while you were in diapers. Heck, I was still in diapers when I was spinning the good ol' bottle. It all began just like this . . .

The only thing greater than my love for the stoop and the toilet was my love for Vicki. Vicki was an older woman who lived on the second floor of our brownstone. She lived right next to the toilet. How convenient. I don't really remember what Vicki looked like, but she must have been fine, because I was in love with her. I could not even say her name, but that was my woman. Whenever Vicki and her boyfriend would play around or have an argument, I would hear them. Then I would crawl down those stairs, so that I could stand in her hallway and yell, "You leave my Bicki alone! Hear me! You leave my Bicki alone!" The only thing I do remember is that Vicki would always come out from her apartment, swoop me up, nestle me close to her bosom. Ahh, true love. Sometimes she would take me back upstairs and sometimes she would let my stay with her in her apartment. To this day **I still love a woman to swoop me and nestle me close to her bosom.** Beautiful full bosoms. I love 'em. Thanks, Bicki. I wonder what ever happened to old Bicki. I wonder if she knows what I have made of myself. I would sure like to thank her for the inspiration to achieve. Hey, maybe she would even nestle me again for old times' sake. I would like that.

Anyway, as you can see, I was a mack in diapers, but it wasn't until I got much older that I had my first real experience with the femme fatale. When we got to be fifteen or sixteen we started playing run, catch, and kiss with the girls. Kids today don't do nothing. I had to be fourteen or fifteen when I lost my virginity, and that's only because my oldest brother forced it on me. "'Cause there would be no homosexuality in our household." My father was a very homophobic man. Every time I was with him and he saw what he considered a "faggot," he would spit on the ground and say, "You ain't gonna be no faggot." Then he would punch me in the chest. (*Boom!*)

So of course my brothers became like Nazis, and their mission was to wipe out all traces of homosexuality in our household. My brothers would ask me, "Do you have a girlfriend?" I'd say, "Nah. I don't like no girls." Then they would beat my ass. So I told them that I did the hoochie coochie with some girl even though I hadn't done a damn thing. Then one day they said, "How do you do it? Where do you put it?" I would tell them that the girl put it in. They said I was lying, so they went and got me a girl, a girl from school. She took me downstairs and put it in for me. I did what I thought I was supposed to be doing. I pushed in and pulled out until I came and that was it. I thought I busted a blood vessel or something. I can remember coming upstairs and asking my brothers what was the pus that came out of my private. They laughed at me so hard. They laughed for days 'cause they knew I didn't know what I was doing. I liked the way it felt, but I didn't know what happened.

I want to thank my folks for a proper church upbringing. Ain't no place better to meet girls.

It got much, much better after that. How about you, Dre? What were your early spin the bottle days like?

I had an older brother who could tell you all about sex. I listened to parts of the stories Fred told and I used my imagination for the rest. At one point we used to think that to make love to a woman, all you had to do was get to her belly button. That was it. You were home free. Imagine a bunch of twelve-year-old kids running around a party—all the guys sitting there just looking for the belly buttons. You just get to a girl and try to figure out how could you get her to show you her belly button. **"Come on, show me the belly button."** One thing that would really freak us out was if the belly button was sticking out! We'd go, "Uh-oh, this ain't a girl!"

Young Dre on the prowl for belly buttons.

My first sexual experience was at a sleepover with my cousin Cindy, some of her friends and myself. I think her name was Karen. Anyhow, there was a bunch of us and we had a sleepover at my cousin's house. We all slept in a big roll-out bed. Boys and girls together. Of course we played our games before we went to bed. We were twelve and thirteen at the time; you know things were going on. We played the fart game every night before we went to bed. Each person would take a turn farting and we would see who could stay under the sheet the longest. The fart game could last all night if you were good at farting. If you had a good meal of beans, you could fart all night long. Anyway, we'd be in our pajamas and stuff, and I never wore pajamas as a child. Never. I would always have to sleep damn near naked. That was just the way it was. So my aunt keeps running up and down and says, "I'm telling you kids to be quiet!" My aunt is nice, the nicest, but when she gets mad, you know she's mad. "It's past your bedtime, now stop that bla, bla, bla up there!" So one of my cousin's friends, Karen, is like really cool. She's nice and we got that **little kiss-kiss thing going on** and all of a sudden, "You're making too much noise. Okay, all the boys in one room and all the girls in the other room. Now!" Auntie broke it up. It would get real quiet and you'd hear, uh, uh, uh, uh, uh, uh, uh as we were switching places, so my cousin switched with some-body and Karen came into my room. I think it was my cousin and this other girl were in the next room and they were naked. The lights were out, but you could see their silhouettes by the light of the moon. We're saying to ourselves, "Hey, that ain't the fart game! Hmmm. What game are they playing? You know, like, aha, that's something different." My older cousin and some girl were doing it on the bed. I was like, "Whoa!" So Karen and I walk into the other room and there's—couples naked there and they're doing the same thing. And we go, "Hey, that's not a bad idea." Of course my aunt didn't know what was goin' on. So we decided that the next night would be our turn. So kids are smart enough to wait.

We could look out the window for the signal—my aunt's light to go out. The light went out and we would wait a little bit and then she'd be asleep. So we would get up that night and ask ourselves, How are we going to do this? When you get right down to it, kids can really do just about anything they set their minds to do. I get over to the other bed and I'm being suave and cool and sophisticated like I can be. We're talking and touching. Just a little necking on the chin. You know, you're smooth. You're fine. You're doing your thing as a kid and eventually skin hits. *Smack!* And you touch IT! **The IT where you**

never touched a girl before and you go ooh and somewhere between that first erection and reality, IT all comes together! That you don't know what the hell to do. Just sit there and Hah! Hah, hah, and she's kissing you like ah hah and then like the top is off and you are sitting there in your drawers with an erection and you are sitting there going, "What do I do?" And you look down and see the belly button and you go, "I got it! The belly button!" So you look at the belly button and you touch and everything and sit there and you are perfectly positioned 'cause your, you know—and she sits there and you . . . Don't even take off your underwear. You just sit down on her belly and imitate what you saw your cousin doin' and you really hump the hell out of her stomach and you do it like for eight, nine minutes and you . . . It's feeling good . . . And you, you . . . Don't even come. You don't come. You're not coming at all. It's really more like ah hah and she looks at you and you look at her and you go, "This was good. We should do this again." And then you fall asleep. She puts her nightie on and you all fall asleep . . . When you wake up to your aunt. Your aunt! She's up and in the bathroom, and then in the other room . . . And I go back in my memory and I laugh at that moment and I say, "I didn't even know what I was trying to do or not do, but it was so much fun tryin' to get there."

THE BIG BACKACHE ERA

NINETEEN eighty-one was the year that *should* have been the best year of my life. I was about to turn eighteen, I was about to become a man, and I was about to graduate from August Martin High School that same year.

Instead of being happy with all the year 1981 was about to promise, I found myself faced with disaster.

During a routine physical, the doctor diagnosed me with having a disease called spinal scoliosis. For those of you who don't know what scoliosis is, it is a curvature of your spinal cord. As you get older, if it is not corrected, your spinal cord just curves more and more. In the long run, as you become older, it can cause respiratory problems and even cause you to walk hunched over.

Needless to say, I was *devastated* when I received the news of my condition. This meant that I would have to have *major surgery* on my spinal cord (you can just imagine the risk involved in that), miss several months of high school, miss the entire *senior year,* and be trapped in a plaster *body cast* for the entire summer! *Shit!!!* Senior year is supposed to be the best year of high school. All the special days, the senior trip, the senior prom, all would have to be missed by me. Who the fuck wants to spend the best year of high school in a body cast? *Nobody!!!!*

The doctor, Dr. Graham, informed my parents and me that I couldn't and shouldn't wait until later to have my operation because of the severity of my curvature. So in April 1981, I entered in the Hospital for Joint Diseases. It took the doctors twelve hours to complete my operation. After my operation I was moved into the intensive care unit for close monitoring. Man, I had tubes coming out of me from everywhere. I had tubes coming out of my nose from down my throat, two IVs in each arm, and a tube inserted into the head of my penis. That tube was there so that I could use the bathroom, see; I was on bed rest, and I couldn't get up and walk around for at least three weeks.

All in all I spent three months in the hospital and nine months in that damn body cast. And boy, did that cast itch like hell during those long, hot summer months. It also fucked up my *sex life!!!* The cast was constructed so that I only had room enough to move my bowels. It went from the top of my neck all the way down to the top of my waistline. **In other words, not much room for fucking!!** It also had what we called a window cut out in the middle around my stomach so that I could use a hanger bottom (the cardboard part) to scratch my stomach and my back!! But you know what? I never once let it get me down!! I tried to do all the normal things that I could. My mother thought I was crazy!! When I was supposed to be at home on bed rest, I would just walk up and down the block by holding onto the fences. After a time I learned how to roller-skate, play basketball, and even sit up in a car, which was really rather difficult. I went through it all. But I survived!! And I was there to coach my sister Sonya through it when she had to have the same operation. You know, it's kinda ironic that, twelve years later, my daughter Tiffany has to have the same operation. I feel for her. And I'm afraid—I mean, she's only twelve years old. At least I was eighteen and a lot more mentally ready to handle the situation. Luckily, I'll be there to coach her through the whole thing too. Oh well, I guess it just *runs in the family!!!!!*

HE, SHE, AND SHIM

WE'RE much more sophisticated now than we were back in our spin-the-bottle days. We've definitely matured. We know the belly button is *not* the way to go anymore. We have a lot more to say on a lot more serious issues concerning men, women, and other people who feel they don't fit in either one of these categories.

HE

WHEN HE GETS THE FEELIN', ED NEEDS SAFE SEXUAL HEALING

"When I get that feeling, I want sexual healing." Marvin Gaye wrote that dynamite song.

I want to talk about sex right now. I have to tell you straight up that I am an admitted sex fiend. I love sex. If I could have sex every single day . . . Oh boy! I adore having sex. You know, guys are different from women. With women you have to, well, most of the time you'll want to know the guy. Maybe you'll see a guy walking down the street and he can be fine as hell with a nice body and everything and look like an Adonis, Brad Pitt, Wesley Snipes, or I don't give a damn who. But most of the time if a woman had any kind of morals whatsoever, she wants to know the guy before she sleeps with him. Women most of the time want to know your last name or they want to know something about you before they sleep with you.

Guys, we don't give a damn. If a woman's got a good face, nice tits, nice ass, and we want to sleep with her, we don't have to know her name. We don't have to know anything about her. I believe that women want sex just as much as men do. But with men it's just instant gratification that we're looking for. We're looking for that instant get-off to get that one great orgasm. We don't even have to know the woman. She could leave, get up, put her clothes on, and walk out of the hotel room or out of your house or wherever you are. But with men it's just that instant gratification. I don't think that all men that fool around on their wives fool around because they don't love their wives. Don't get me wrong—I think they really love their wives. It's just the conquering principle. To have that great sex and the variety of it all makes men do what they do.

But me, I'm an admitted sex fiend. I love to have sex and, if I could be so blunt, I'd say I just love to fuck. I love beautiful women. Sometimes I think that's going to be my downfall because I love beautiful women so much. I love sex. I've had some great one-night stands with some wonderful women, and they know who they are.

"When I get that feeling, I need sexual healing." The best thing that I like to do when it comes to sex is I like it when a woman just talks dirty. I think most men like that. I think most men want a good wife, an intelligent woman who can hold her own, a good mother to their children, and a whore in the bedroom. Excuse me, I just think that most men really want that. I think I can speak for Black men when I say Black men want that. I couldn't tell you what white men want because I'm not a white man. Most Black men that I've talked to in my lifetime want that. They want a woman that's intelligent, a good mother who can cook, and a nasty whore in the bedroom. They want to try things men like. There's probably just about only one fantasy a Black woman couldn't live up to in the bedroom. We want threesomes. We want to be with two women at the same time. It's the fantasy of most men. It's the God's honest truth. Most men want to have more than one woman in the bed at the same time at least one time in their lives. I think it's just a man thing.

But the bad thing about sex right now is that that shit is too damn dangerous! I mean, why did it have to happen when I'm in my sexual prime, when I'm ready to do the things I enjoy doing? I enjoy oral sex. I enjoy going down on a woman and making her squirm and doing the things that make women want to climb a wall and scream my name. But nowadays you might die.

Just recently during Spring Break '95, I found out the Eazy-E, one of the founding members of the rap group N.W.A, was in the hospital in Los Angeles dying of AIDS. For those of you who never heard of Eazy-E, N.W.A has been all over the paper for songs like "Fuck tha Police," and their group's name even caused controversy—it stand for Niggaz With Attitude. He was famous for rap, but he was also a businessman, a political figure, and an activist for the gang-war truce in Los Angeles.

It really makes you afraid of having sex. It's like, damn, when I'm at my sexual peak I can't get my groove on and it really, really scares the shit out of me. I was with guys from the rap world and the R&B world such as Naughty by Nature, Pepa of Salt-n-Pepa, Queen Latifah, and Shakim of the Flava Unit. We were all together sitting around talking about this thing that's touching us because nobody from our circle (not even Magic Johnson, that's a whole different circle than the rap world, R&B music world) had been diagnosed with having AIDS—you know, dying of AIDS right in front of our faces.

You can't even trust a condom. Even with a condom, what about all them other things you like to do, like oral sex? You can get this AIDS giving oral sex. You can't even enjoy yourself anymore. You can't even get your swerve on or your groove on, as we like to say. It's scary; it can kill ya.

Somebody better wake up out there and find a cure for this, and the government better stop spending so much money on the military, because there will be no people around because we'll all be dead of AIDS. We need to get it together!

The next time you get that feeling for some sexual healing and it ain't safe, get a container of Häagen-Dazs ice cream, take a cold shower, and go the fuck to bed!

ED LOVER'S
TIPS [RECIPE] FOR A HOT NIGHT OF LOVIN'!!!!!

1. One jar of *honey!!!!!*

2. Six cubes of *ice!!!*

3. One *king-size bed* (satin sheets are optional!!!)

4. One or two pair of *handcuffs or some rope!!!!!* (the choice is yours!!)

5. *The greatest slow jams in the world* (cassette or CD is also optional!!)

6. *Incense* ('cause you don't want to smell the funk before its time!)

7. *Satin panties or boxer shorts or even briefs* (for those men who wear punk panties!)

8. A long, hot, steamy, soapy *bath or shower!!* ('cause, *oh,* see *#6!!!*)

9. The *right person or people* (depending on how you get down, of course!!)

10. This is the *most* important thing that you must have. I cannot stress this enough.

For that perfect evening of hot lovin' you must possess this one crucial thing:
A VIVID IMAGINATION!!!!!!

DON'T FORGET TO HAVE A GOOD TIME AND PRACTICE SAFE SEX!!! ENJOY!!!!!!

ED? A DADDY?

think women do a good job raising kids on their own. But a boy definitely needs a male figure around. It's the same thing with a man who has custody of his little girl; he can't teach her how to be a woman. Even if parents are not together, they have to get along for the children's sake. They have to set rules together. There can't be different rules for each household. My daughter follows the same rules at my house that she follows at her mother's house. And when her mother moved in with her boyfriend, I had to tell him that I discipline my daughter because she's mine, not his. A lot of fathers today aren't doing right by their kids and neither are some of the mothers.

Having a child is a serious commitment, but we don't have any control over that as a man because we get tricked. The woman says, "Don't wear a condom because I'm on the pill." But then when she gets pregnant, everything changes. She wants the baby and you're not ready for one. I don't think it's right for a woman to try to trap a man into having a baby. That's when I think it's okay for a woman to have an abortion. I think if a man tells a woman, "I don't want a child," and she decides to have it anyway, she should take care of it herself. He didn't want it, so don't go suing for child support and chasing him down, because he told you he didn't want the child from day one.

I think a man should take care of his kids because children need a father figure. But we know who's holding the determining factor. The woman is holding the determining factor. If you know a child needs a mother and a father, and you know that the man is not gonna be there for you, if he told you, "I'm not checkin' for this baby," why bring the baby into the world? Just because you want one? If you wait, you could probably have a baby with a man that wants you and a child. I think a lot of women are too damn young when they make those decisions. I've been in a situation with my daughter's mother. I thought she was on the pill. Then she broke out and left and went to Barbados when she knew she was pregnant. She didn't tell me she was pregnant, and she went to Barbados for eight months and came back pregnant and said it was my baby. I asked her later on, when my daughter was 'bout five or six, "Why did you do that?" I think she thought she would have me if she had a baby. We're not together now, never have been since then, and never will be. But I love my daughter.

At first I was like I really should say fuck it, but I wasn't raised that way. My father taught us that if you make it, you take care of it, regardless of the consequences. I guess that stems from my two older brothers, Kelvin and Larry. They're not my father's biological sons, but he raised all four of us. My sister Sonya and I are the only ones from my parents. Kelvin and Larry have a different father. My father loved my mother, so the kids came along with it, and he raised all four of us like everybody was his. I've seen a picture of my oldest brother Kelvin's father. His name is Melvin. He lives down south somewhere. He hasn't seen my brother in about twenty-eight years. He told my mom that he wants to come up and see his grandchildren. My brother said, "I don't want that man stepping foot in my front door because my *real* father"—meaning my dad—"died twelve years ago."

Any man can be a biological daddy, but it takes a real man to be a father. I think both sexes have problems and we need to get ourselves together. But the women have the determining factor on whether or not to have a child. So women have to think a lot harder about who they're getting ready to have a baby with and whether or not he's going to be there. Even if they're not together, a child needs to know that both parents care about them and is going to be there for him/her. I don't think my daughter's mother made it any easier by going and having another baby by another guy after that. To me, that's not a great example for my daughter. The worst thing about it though is that I have two daughters and both of their mothers did the same thing. I felt like my oldest daughter's mother had Tiffany to try to trap me because once she got it in her head that we wasn't going to be together, she moved on. She's still a pain, it seems like she tries to go to court every time I get a raise. But trying to be with me is not there anymore. I would think not after twelve years. But she was never really my girlfriend. She was just someone to hang with when I was home from school. She was never really someone I loved. But she became somebody I cared about, and I was dumb enough to believe she was on the pill and I didn't use a condom. My father had already given me the condom speech too, and my oldest brother Kelvin had just had a son. Little Kelvin was six years old. As soon as my father found out that Kelvin wasn't committed to his son's mother, I got taken around the corner for the old condom speech. "Boy, I know you're having sex. I know it. Don't lie to me. I know you're having sex. So, here," and he gave me a box of condoms. "You need me to show you how to put them on." I was like, "No, dad, I don't need you to show me how to put them on. I'm straight." My dad told me to wear a condom all the time to protect myself from everything, but I didn't listen. If I knew back then what I know now, I would have worn one every time and not because of my daughter. I love my daughter. I'm so glad God gave her to me. But because of AIDS and stuff because it could have a ten-year incubation period in your body. I could have got it when I was twenty-two or sixteen.

My youngest daughter's mother was different. I loved her. I wanted to marry her and I wanted to have a baby. I told her I would marry her and stop playing music with the band I was in and join the air force, but she was in another relationship. They're more mature now. I used to say that I had daughters by two crazy-ass women, because when she was pregnant by me, her boyfriend was in jail. They must have had sex when she went upstate to visit him. She told him it was his kid and then she married him. But I knew it was mine. When my daughter was first born she let me see my daughter. She let me play Daddy while he was in jail. She kept saying she was going to tell him. "I'm going to tell him. I'm going to tell him. I'm going to tell him." But her boyfriend had been in jail for violent crimes, so she didn't want to tell him. She was scared of him. She never got around to telling him for a long time, and she had a son by him. Whenever he went to jail, I could play Daddy. But when he came home, she'd take my daughter away. I got tired of it and I told her, "Don't bother me, because I'm going to do what I've got to do. I know what direction I'm going in. If you want to, follow this man who doesn't know where he's going. He just goes back and forth to jail, back and forth to jail; he's never gonna change." I knew I was going to miss my daughter because she's a part of me. But I knew one day she was going to ask where her father was and her mother would have to come up with an answer. It's sad because once I had my daughter and I was taking her to get a pair of shoes, she said, "You know what, Daddy, I'm lucky because I have two daddies." She was about three years old. She said, "I got you and I got my other daddy." I said, "You don't have two daddies. I'm your father and I'm your only father and I love you."

She used to always go home and watch me on *Yo! MTV Raps,* and he knew me and my daughter's mother had an affair. He'd sit there in the living room and my daughter would say, "There's my daddy on TV." My daughter's mother's cousin would be around and she would say, "Oh! she loves him so much, she's just playing. She doesn't know what she's talking about. She's young." But she always knew I was her father. Now he's in jail, doing something like forty years, and the judge told him he'd never see daylight again.

My daughter was going through a lot of problems in school. Well, it all came down to the fact that all the other little kids in school had a daddy and she didn't. She started lying, not doing her homework, and fighting other kids. They thought something was psychologically wrong with her. They took her to a psychologist and she broke down. She wanted to know why her father on TV and on the radio didn't love her and why her other daddy was in jail. The psychologist asked her who her daddy was.

Finally her mother told him that my daughter was not his child. Of course, he lost it and he threatened her. She should have told him from day one. She finally told me my little girl was going through all this trouble, and even though I had washed my hands of the whole thing . . . but the way I was raised by James and Viola, I said to myself, "That's your child. Go get her and take care of her." So I went out there and I saw her. I hadn't seen her since she was three years old and now she's eight. As soon as I came back into her life and she knew that Daddy was there and I loved her, everything was all right. Her grades picked up. She does well now.

Tiffany and Chanelle, those are my girls. I guess her not being with me was God's way of steering me into the path that He wanted me to take. I guess He was taking me away from that. If He hadn't, I would have been in the air force and MTV would have never happened. Hot 97 would have never happened, this whole book would have never happened. I was ready for a military career.

I took my daughters to Disney World in December '94. They didn't even know each other, and it's funny how the older one fell into the older-sister thing. They live so far apart. I wish I could have them together more often. It was good to have both of my little girls together at the same time. I wish I could not have the headaches of the mothers and just have the kids. I wish I could find a woman to have a kid and just give it to me. My father was there for me. You've got to make sacrifices for your kids. You've got to be there for your kids.

My Girls, Tiffany and Chanelle.

A lot of things are wrong with this world.
A lot of the conservative opinions that I fought against I now find them to be correct. African Americans don't really have family values. I'm a father and I'm not with either of my daughters' mothers. It's weird. The only thing that I can do as a father that's not married to his daughters' mothers is make sure that my daughters know that I love them. You can instill values and morals in your child if you play a part in their lives. I also think the government should play a part, but not the overall or dominating part, in raising our children.

JUST CALL ME DOCTOR LOVE

Romance is the way you act and treat someone you care about as opposed to someone you don't care about. For instance, if you like a woman, you don't go Dutch. "I ordered the shrimp cocktail and a soda, we split the salad, so the rest is on you. No one told you to order from that side of the menu." Romance is special. It's a feeling you have between you and that special person and it's always the hardest thing in a relationship to reinvent and keep fresh and new. You know when the romance dies when you hear someone say, "I cheated because I was bored and you wasn't giving me what I needed." No, you didn't reinvent the romance in your relationship because you were too

. . . It's always the hardest thing in a relationship to reinvent and keep fresh and new.

busy trying to create it elsewhere. You weren't communicating with your mate about your needs and finding out about their needs as well. Infidelity has nothing to do with the act, but it has everything to do with your existing relationship and it was the result of the disparity in that relationship. Don't blame your mate, find out what was lacking, and move on and make sure it doesn't happen again. Romance is doing things because you want to, not because it's expected of you. Spending time and caring for someone.

Washing their feet. Rubbing their backs. Sending flowers for no reason. Singing to your mate on their answering machine. Don't do it because you think it will get you something; do it because you want to do it.

You have to listen to what your mate's likes and dislikes are and try to stay within those parameters. Give them their space and let them be an individual so they can reenter the relationship revived and renewed. Be original. Don't do the same thing over and over again, because it gets tired. Romance is what kept my father and mother together for twenty-seven years until death did them part. They constantly reinvented their romance. Romance is ever changing. Delightful. Happy. Sad. Romance is a fight. Romance understands. Romance is fulfilling. Romance is listening. Now that's a big part. You can hear, but if you don't listen, that's two different worlds. Romance is being able to recognize when you're wrong and being

Romance is doing things because you want to, not because it's expected of you.

able to be flexible. Romance is a rainy night and a sunny day. The difference between romance and love is that romance is the road to love. I've never been with a woman that I've been romantic with that hasn't still called me to this day. Because we were on the road to love, and that's something that will last a lifetime. Romance is the action you take to get love. It's the proving constantly over and over again where your intentions lie towards that person. Once I was so in love with a woman and she told me that I never sent her flowers. That wasn't true, but I said okay. I called the florist and I told him I wanted to literally fill this woman's house with flowers so that everywhere she looked she would see flowers. Needless to say, when she got home she was speechless. She started to cry and then she stopped herself and said, "You didn't have to do this. One flower would've been fine." It's not the magnitude of the act, but it's the thought. Making a card instead of buying a card. Things like that. Let me let all you women know men feel the hurt and pain from the loss of love just the same as women do. We sit home and hear those songs too and then we start singing along. "Although, we've gone to the end of the road, I can't let you go" or "Oh God, give me a reason, I'm down on bended, down on bended knee . . ." It hurts us too! We feel the same pain; we just react differently. We wonder if something's wrong with us when we do all the right things and that special person still isn't interested in you. It's not just men doggin' out women here, because men get dogged out too.

I'm not a hypocrite to any woman I'm with, because if I can sit back and watch a woman walk by in a provocative outfit and *ooh* and *ahh* about how good she looks and then I turn around and see my woman walk out of the house the same way, I can't grab her and tell her to go put some clothes on. I have to say, "Go do what you're going to do and I hope nothing happens. If somebody puts their hands on you, I'll intervene, but if they yell and shout and talk, there's nothing I can do because that's being hypocritical." You can't like something and then tell your woman, No, you can't dress like that. I'm secure in myself and my relationships and that's the key. The only time I may become insecure in a relationship is if I happen to get involved with a vindictive woman, or a woman shows that she isn't trustworthy. The Penelope Pitstops of the world, women that want to be saved and I'm Dudley Do-Right. I think I'm a nut.

Sometimes the best woman or man for you could be right under your nose. That special girl or guy friend you love hanging out with could be the one. Some people deny it, but the reason they're together as friends is because they're attracted to each other. Believe me, if you put the right oil in the right place at the right time, you'll have fried fish every time! It don't matter who don't think they can't get fried, they'll be fried nearly close to burned spilling over the plate all the time!

ED LOVER'S
FIVE THINGS THAT TURN WOMEN <u>ON!!!!</u>

I don't have a college degree, but when it comes to *women,* I have studied them extensively. So I hope you find this information useful to you. It took me years of mental and sometimes oral study to come to these conclusions. Well, here it goes:

1. **Intellect and Sincerity.** Speak to women like the beautiful creatures that they are. You don't have to be a Harvard graduate, but you also don't have to say "You know what I'm sayin'?" forty-five times within a ten-minute conversation.

2. **Good Hygiene.** Brush your teeth, clean under your finger- and toenails, cut your hair at least once every two weeks, etc., etc. (Women notice these things whether you believe it or not.)

3. **Always Smell Nice.** It doesn't have to be the most expensive cologne, and it also doesn't have to be Brut by Fabergé. And remember, fellas, never overdo it!! She doesn't need to smell you before you come around the corner.

4. **Personality and Employment**. If you happen to have been blessed by being handsome, *nothing* turns a woman *off* more than conceit and snootiness. Don't just talk about yourself all evening. Be responsive to her needs and learn to listen for a change. One more thing to remember, fellas: Romance without finance is a nuisance. Get a job!!

5. **Try to Stay in Some Kind of Shape.** Women *hate* it when a man has a considerable amount of *dick do!!* That's when your stomach sticks out further than your DICK DO!!! You don't have to be Mr. Olympia, but try to stay in some kind of decent shape.

 IF NONE OF THE ABOVE PERTAINS TO YOU,
I REALLY FEEL SORRY FOR YA, BROTHER!!!

ED'S LOVE NOTES

WOMEN have more inhibitions if they're sober. They're more likely to say, "We shouldn't be doing this." Men will do it any time and any place. A woman could see a good-looking man with a nice body on the street and say, "Ooh, I want to get to know him." Men don't care. They see a nice ass and a nice chest and they say, "Ooh, I want to fuck her." They don't even have to know your last name. Women are more connected spiritually and emotionally to sex than men are. That's why when a man fools around, it has nothing to do with a spiritual connection 90 percent of the time. It's a dick thang and women will never understand it. I figured out women are more emotional with it because women have internal sexual organs and a man has an external sexual organ. A man is putting something inside a woman and that's internal, so they have to be emotional with that. That's why I think fags are so emotional—because they have something going up inside them. Of course, that's the exit ramp and that's why they become womanlike.

I do think men can be faithful, but the men that do cheat, they don't have emotional ties to sex. Don't get me wrong; I'm not justifying any man cheating on his woman. I'm just giving a basis for how some men think.

WOMEN cheat because they're not getting what they need from their man either emotionally or physically at home. If you find a woman and she's got a man and he can't make her have an orgasm like she wants to have an orgasm and another man does, she's hooked, whipped—call her what you want—but he's got her. She might not leave her man, but she'll keep the other man on the side. I've had married women before and I've asked them, "Why are you with me if you love your husband so much?" They say, "Because you make me feel like I need to feel and he doesn't." I think it's a matter of communication. I think it's a matter of a man tapping into his woman's needs. Men tend to talk *at* women, they don't talk *to* them. Because we come home and we're dealing with this everyday struggle of just being a Black man in America, we forget who the backbone of the Black family is. It has always been our Black women. We forget, so we tend to talk at them not to them. Even in general conversation, even just meeting a woman, we talk at them not to them to find out about them, and that communication barrier is there. So she's not getting what she wants emotionally.

On the other hand, **women have got to stop looking for Mr. Perfect.** Mr. Perfect doesn't exist. Even when they get into a relationship, they'll put up with flaws that they know they don't like because they think they can change it. They say, "Oh, it'll be different when we get married. He's gonna stop smoking cigarettes. He's going to stop smoking weed. He's gonna stop cursing. He's gonna stop all of that and I'm gonna get him to go to church." Well, if that ain't the kind of man you've got then, that ain't the kind of man you're gonna have. You can't change a person to that extent and I think women tend to think they can do that.

I don't think most men want to get married. I think they get married to please their women because they love them and don't want to lose them. I never met a man who had the idea to get married, at least out of the men I know. I think men are scared of commitment.

In a car, at a museum, the first step is always attraction. Look at her—it can be physical attraction all the time. Look at him. Ah, damn, he's cute. Whatever. Wow, she's got a nice body. She's got a nice ass. She's got nice tits. She's cute. She's got nice eyes. I don't care what it is, the first step is always attraction. You're

And Pepa still looks fine!

attracted to him, he's attracted to you. You meet him in a club, the music's pumpin', she's sweating. Her body's dynamite. The first step is always attraction 'cause even when I used to like Pepa from Salt-n-Pepa, my first thing with her was attraction. I used to watch the videos and go, "Damn! Pepa's fine, dynamite, nice everything." The first step is always attraction.

The second step is after you meet the person, it's infatuation. You call all the time, exchange phone numbers, make sure the person's not a freakin' idiot or some kind of stalker, and she's got some sort of common sense to her—it's infatuation. You like to talk to her, you really want to talk to her. Every time you turn around you're thinking about her—that's not love, that's infatuation. You call all the time, you go out. You like being with them, you hang out, you go to the beach. You know, you do what you gotta do, like the time Salt-n-Pepa came down for Spring Break. At the time, I was really infatuated with Pepa. I sent her a teddy bear and roses—you know, you do things out of the ordinary. And on the way back they needed a ride, and I live in Jersey City, and I drove them all the way to Queens. Just so I could be in the presence of this woman, I gave them a ride all the way to Queens—that's a long haul. I was infatuated with her. I don't think that she knew that I liked her on such a grand scale, but I did.

Now the third step in any relationship is love. Two people figure out they really love each other when you pretty much can't bear the thought of being without that other person. Love is more than infatuation. It's when you know that if that person died or if you died that your life would never be the same.

I never really got to that point of love with Pepa because I don't really think that she liked me. I don't think that I'm her kind of guy. Now I pretty much feel like an asshole after I went through everything. But it was all cool. I mean, we're friends to this day. She was with my man Treach. That's my man from Naughty by Nature, so it's all good.

But the person that you love, you can't bear the thought of being without this person in your lifetime. I don't mean that *Fatal Attraction*–type stuff, but the thought of not being able to share your hopes, dreams, successes, and failures with this person leaves you empty. Yes, women, us guys have that same empty feeling you have when it feels like you've lost the one you love. But let's proceed.

Now, I've been in love on several occasions. The first time I was in love, I think it was when I was in the third grade. I was in love with this girl that had a green sweater. Actually, I think it was more like #2-infatuation. I just went to day camp so I could see her. She had those little stubby nubbies on her chest, which I guess in those days passed as breasts for me. She had these little stubby nubbies and she was real cute. I don't even remember her name. I just remember that green sweater that she had at day camp, and I always went to day camp because of that girl.

The second time I was in love, I was in love with a girl—let's just call her Barbara. I was in love with Barbara, and Barbara broke my heart because I found her in bed with another man. Really I did. I came over one night after hanging out with the fellas, I turned my key in her apartment door and she was in bed with another man. That love moved into the next category, which I'll get at right after I finish this love thing.

The third time I was in love I was with this wonderful woman named Tee. We were together for many wonderful years. We even had a house in Virginia, three dynamite kids (her biological kids, my heart-lights). Terrence and Tyshawn, identical twin boys, and Terri. We even had two doggies. But I fucked up. Tee was one of the best things that ever happened to me. But I wasn't really ready for a serious marriage-style commitment and I fooled around on her and broke her heart. I would just like to take this moment to say I'm sorry to Tee.

The next time I was in love was with this woman named Kim. Kim and I were together for three and a half years. I gave Kim everything she could want, paying her rent and doing everything for her, but I never supported her. You might scratch your head and think, How didn't you support her? Well, I didn't give her a chance to explore her own interests and grow. You see, I wanted to control her because I had been hurt so many times before. One day it all came tumbling down. We had a big fight because I thought she was fooling around on me. We said foolish things and it got heated for a while until we just couldn't get along. That love almost turned to hate.

When you love a person and they do you wrong and break your heart, you hate. I hated Barbara and Kim for a long time, and Tee hated me. We all really had to learn to get over that hate and learn to forgive. Until you forgive that person, you won't be able to go on and have healthy relationships. That's the problem we have as young men and women nowadays. We get out of one relationship and try to hop into another one so quickly. I read somewhere that for every year you went out with a person you should wait a month's time before you start seeing someone else. That's about how long it will take you to heal from the wounds of that relationship. Some people don't even give it a week before they start seeing a new person, and they bring all the pain and anger of the previous relationship to the new one. It took me a while to realize this, but now I understand. Kim and I spoke recently, and then we saw each other after being separated for eight months. We both healed and now we're back together again. If we didn't take that time to heal we might have lost each other forever. I love her and now we can start all over again and do it right!

M e and Kim (a.k.a. Pootie Mac)

See, **love is like shit. It makes your life bloom** and everybody needs love and we all want to love and be in love. But you really never know when you might step in a pile of dog shit and you never know when you might step in love because you can go from being attracted to somebody, then being infatuated with someone, to loving somebody, to hating them just like that—with a snap of your fingers. So you just remember: The next time love comes around, make sure you're wearing high boots above your thigh, because the shit can be kind of high.

MORE THAN A BANG

WE'RE about to have a bachelor party. We're bachelors and we're gonna have a party. Why we always got to be walking the last mile just to have a bachelor party? We think you certainly can have a few practice runs before the big day. We don't disrespect women, but we've been put in a couple of situations where it became incredibly hard to "Just say no!" In the minds of the general public, people think women are these innocent creatures who just fall prey to the dogs of the world. That's a lie! We've met some unscrupulous women in our day who would do basically anything—and I mean anything—to sleep with a celebrity. Here are just a few of the tales . . .

ONCE a fraternity basically gave us a girl as part of our salary. That was in the rider. It's like, you're gonna get this and a girl. "What do you mean, 'a girl'?" "At the end of the night. You made it dynamite for us, you came and partied with us, we're sending you a girl."

They're like, "Yeah, one of our soros [sorority sisters]." So they sent this girl and we're like, "Damn, we're not trying to go to jail for touching this girl up." This was prior to the Mike Tyson and Tupac incidents.

We were on the *Yo! MTV Raps* college tour, so we had adjoining rooms. We had two rooms. It was me, Dre, and our MTV boys. We're all in the room with this girl (after they sent her in) and everybody's scared to touch her.

Let us tell you, a book ain't nothin' like its cover. Man, she looked like she was the perfect college student. She had glasses on and her books in hand. She had a package, though. Her package was right. We're like, "I can't do this, I can't do this. This looks like my sister." So we're all sitting there going, "No, we can't do this."

You know who got his pants down first. Hello, Ed!!!! Ed was first. Think about it: How many men would've said no? **She took care of the whole crew, all four of us**. Then she came to the show that night, sat in the front smiling and waving.

WE respect women that respect themselves. If they don't respect themselves, who will? Women are the most beautiful things in the world and they're the most complex. Carry yourselves that way and demand respect! We live in an opportunistic world and people will try to get all that they can, so all you women out there need to protect yourselves and be yourselves. Don't go along with the gang, because when you're down and out with AIDS, where will they be?

ED'S FAVORITE FLAVAS

I had a white girlfriend when I was in my early teens. But she wasn't what I would call a white girl. But she was a white girl because she grew up in the projects with the rest of us. She wasn't the ordinary stereotypical white girl. She wasn't like, "Oh my God! Like, I've got to go get my nails done," you know, accompanied by the all-too-familiar hair toss. Instead she was like, "Yo!! Wassup, nigga? What's going down?" She was the only white person that I've ever heard Black people would let say, "Yo, what's up, nigga?" Everybody knew Nikki. She was Black but she wasn't Black. It's like a Puerto Rican. It's almost like people said, "She's not white, she's a Puerto Rican who doesn't speak Spanish."

I just don't like white girls. I don't look at them as attractive. I don't look at girls like Julia Roberts, Christy Turlington, or Cindy Crawford. I've been around Cindy Crawford and she does nothing for Ed. Maybe white boys think she's dynamite. And, Pamela Anderson with those super tits, well, I need some backside with my woman. I need some butt.

I like Puerto Rican women. To me, they're half and half who speak Spanish. Puerto Rican woman are dynamite. The Asian women I've seen never have a frame I'm interested in—you know, like Black women's curves, the hips, the legs, those powerful thighs, and the hips.

Everybody has a right to their own personal opinion. There are white people out there that don't want their cousins or what-have-you to marry people of different races. That's all right with me. It's funny, though, because when we see them, they're the ones sitting up onstage on these talk shows, the Black women in the audience will get up and say, "That ain't right. You shouldn't be racist like that. You should let her marry whoever she wants to. Just because she wants to be with a Black man that doesn't mean anything." But put that same woman in the audience when a Black man onstage says, "I don't check for Black women. I only marry white women." These same Black women would have a fit. They would say, "What's wrong with you? You know what your problem is? You just can't handle a strong Black woman." So they don't know what they want.

Sometimes I feel like that too. I'm like, Why do I feel like they're doing something wrong by having a white woman? I think I feel like that because I still think that white people oppress Black people in this country so, unfortunately, I can't see being with one. Also, since we have so many problems as Black people, we need to work on our relationships to keep the sense of family and community alive. I know that I may sound a little stereotypical, but I definitely know what I want. I always tell my friends if they're thinking about going out with a woman of another race, more power to you. Just care for each other and you will be able to work everything else out in time.

ED LOVER'S

FIVE THINGS GUARANTEED TO TURN WOMEN <u>OFF</u>!!!!

1. **Bad Breath.** This is guaranteed to get you nothing but dissed!!!

2. **Corny Pickup Lines.** Intelligent women *hate* this shit!!! A definite *no-no!!*

3. **Rotten Teeth.** Don't even bother to open up if you have *yuck mouth!!!*

4. **Touching without Permission.** Don't touch it if you don't want to pull back a

BLOODY **STUMP**!!! Women I know hate to be pulled on, hate to have their asses

grabbed, etc., etc.

5. **Never Say the Words "Bitch"** and *"Hello" in the Same Sentence!!!*

Need I say *MORE?!!!*

SHIM

DRE'S FIRST GLIMPSE IN THE CLOSET

WHEN you grew up, homosexuality wasn't as open, but there was always one openly gay guy. Our guy was nicknamed Mr. Sensitivity, Michael Jackson's twin. All the girls loved him, he always dressed the best, he was always neat, and all the girls just loved him. They'd say, "He's so sensitive. He's so sweet. He really understands us." I was stupid enough to think if I played the gay thing, the girls would come flocking. That thought lasted for about twelve seconds. The first eleven seconds were me thinking to myself, "Are you a crazy Black man? What is your problem?" The last one second was me thinking, "Well, it could work."

There was always one in your class and every family has a homosexual. Every family's got one. For us it was my *special* uncle. I'd always say, "How come Uncle Will is always with a guy?" It was Aunt Joanie and Uncle Jim, Uncle Sonny and Aunt Eleanor, Uncle Leon and Aunt Ethel, Uncle William and "Who's the guy named Bill??? Who's this Bill? He's not my uncle. Why is he always with Uncle Will and **why does he wear so much pink?**" My mom would always answer my questions with, "Don't you worry about that, baby. He's Uncle Will's friend. Uncle Will's *special* friend." It just never registered. I loved my Uncle Will and that's all that mattered. His friend was nice too, so I always thought that's what made him *special*.

I'm not threatened by it just as long as it is not forced upon me. Everyone makes their own choice. As for bisexuality, I don't think there is such a thing as bisexuality. Either you're a six-pack or a thumb warmer. But heah, power to the people. If you think you're bisexual, great, but just make sure the heterosexual side is the one you bring on our date.

I can handle everything from homosexuality to even a person considering themselves bisexual, but the one thing I can't understand is cross-dressing. Who are you trying to fool? If that's your thing, cool, but don't try to fool anybody. That's some dangerous shit right there. A man goes to a club and meets this hot woman—because some of them do look better than a lot of women I've seen—and you come on to her/him. You take her/him home and you're prepared to get busy and do your thing and all of a sudden this he/she pulls a Crying Game on me. Well, he would be the only one crying.

Being gay is a choice, and I think anyone who's gay should be proud of their choice. More power to you if that's your thing. I think you should be proud of your preference, but you don't have to wear that sexual preference on your sleeve. I don't go around saying, "I'm proud to be heterosexual." I just am.

C.R.E.A.M.

"CASH RULES EVERYTHING AROUND ME
C.R.E.A.M., GET THE MONEY
DOLLA, DOLLA BILL, Y'ALL."

—Wu-Tang Clan, "C.R.E.A.M."

HOW true is that lyric? "Cash rules everything around me." We think it happens to be very true, unfortunately. Money definitely makes the world go 'round, and we're here to tell you how it changes things and makes things just a little bit different from the times when you didn't have any money.

DRE'S PIGGY BANK

I come from a family that had no money. My grandmother would give me a quarter if I did something nice for the day. You were supposed to just save your quarter in this piggy bank that was bought for you—a big red plastic piggy bank.

I was one of those rare children who understood capitalism from the start and a couple of good episodes of *The Partridge Family* helped support my young philosophy. You see, I always used to have this affinity for Danny Partridge, the one who would be the slick business guy. So I put that quarter in the piggy bank, but I also found a little hole in the bottom of the big thing. Now, I knew I could take the money out. So, being the honest child that I was, I had to put the quarter in the bank and save it for a couple of days. Make sure the bank made noise for a little while and then I would pop out a few of them—pick up a few essential items like comic books, candy, you know, the important stuff—and throw a few IOUs in the bank, and that was my first dealings with credit.

One day my grandmother picked up the piggy bank and shook it and heard all this paper rumpling around. She said, "Well, what is this? Let's see what my baby has saved here." And she pulled out the piece of paper and it said, "I owe twenty-five cents. I owe twenty-five cents, I owe twenty-five cents. I owe twenty-five cents." And she said, "Hey, wait a minute, I thought you had dollars or at least quarters there!"

I admired Danny Partridge so much, I even dressed like him.

So I gave her my immature thoughts about credit, "Well, the fact that I had money to borrow from the bank, Grandma, means that I can replace more quarters for the IOUs, then have more money, and then I can start borrowing all over again." Of course, I got a beating and the little hole was taped over so I couldn't use my credit theory again for a long time.

I feel the same way about money now, which I admit is a shame, but now I don't have to write IOUs anymore. All I have to do is sign my name at the dotted line. I may not get a beating from my grandmother anymore, but I must say I sure do get a beating from those finance charges with the bank (something I forgot to calculate when I was young).

The other bigger system I worked on was the fact that if you ever want to finance something, use your parents. Every one of us have probably used that system as we grew up in life, but me, I've used it more than most.

My grandparents were from Jamaica; my father's side. They were very poor people. I went to Jamaica and saw their home. They had a two-bedroom hut. It was like you opened the door and you looked out into the backyard and the floor was like the ground outside. They grew from that situation with the help of my grandmother working in villas cleaning and doing maid's work. Eventually she ran a maid's service and bonded several of the maids together and then sold her services out to all different villas for vacationing people. Eventually my grandparents bought a store and then started their own little resort. By working hard and sticking together through the good and especially bad times, they brought prosperity to a family that basically started out with nothing.

My grandmother obviously didn't write little notes, "I owe . . ." She had jars, jars all around the house with all kinds of coins in them. I do the same thing now, which is very queer. I have jars all over my house, filled with coins. I have penny jars, I have a quarter jars, nickels, dimes—you name it. I swear to you, at one point when I first moved to my new house I rolled a lot of it up to pay the mortgage. I had like $1,500 in change and I took it all to the bank. It looked as silly as hell, but I went to the bank every other day for about a week because I didn't want to feel stupid. Everyone knew who I was, so I tried to keep a low profile, but on the last day that I finished paying my mortgage with the quarters, one of the tellers who I had probably seen three times that week pulled me to the side and told me not be ashamed, because at least I had the money rolling in.

My grandparents, David Brown Sr. and Adelaide Brown.

HOW MONEY CHANGES SEX

MONEY changes everything. Money changes the way you look. You could be ugly when you don't have no money when you're starting out, then all of a sudden you're good-lookin'. I've seen some ugly celebs with beautiful women.

You don't want people to write about you later on down the line. You worry about your performance. You don't want to mess up the draws or the bed. You worry about your performance more. You don't want people to say you were wack in the sack, so you worry about that.

HOW MONEY CHANGES YOUR ATTITUDE

MONEY changes your patience. If someone's trying to sell you something now and you're spending a lot of money for it, you don't want to hear all of that extra stuff. You know before you sit there and go "I understand if I do this, I make a payment here and save and I don't eat lunch for a week and I put this together so I can do this." Now, I'm like, Brothas, how

much is it? I didn't ask you all of that. I didn't ask you about a payment plan. Don't tell me about a payment plan if I didn't ask you.

You become short with people. Ed went to a jewelry store and he wanted to buy this ring for his mother. Ed got his mother a ring with her birth gem. It was emeralds encrusted in the middle with diamonds all around the ring. He knew how much money he had in his pocket and how much he could afford to spend on the ring. So when he went in the store, he asked how much the ring was. The lady said, "Oh God, that's terribly expensive." Of course, you get the typical Ed response, "I didn't ask you was it expensive. I didn't ask you that. I'm not here with a layaway plan. How much is the ring, Miss?" Automatically because you're Black and you're walking into the store, you can't afford it. That's a nice way of saying it's out of your range.

HOW MONEY CHANGES YOUR SURROUNDINGS

WHEN you didn't have money, all you had in your apartment was that couch you bought from Ikea. The homeboys could come through and put their feet up on your couch. But when you have the $7,000 Ultrasuede sectional in the living room, don't put your feet out on my couch. Don't put your cigarette butts out on my hardwood floor. That carpet cost me $1,500. Please do not wipe your muddy feet on my Persian rug. In that aspect, it always changes you. You should still be able to come around and hang out, but people change towards you. Not the core of homeboys, but sometimes they get a little lax because they know you've got money and you got something in here on this check.

THE DEVIL IN A PINSTRIPE SUIT

MONEY also changes who you know. The first person you meet when you get some money is the Devil in a pinstripe suit. The IRS. The IRS doesn't give a damn how they get it, they want their money. Immediately, right now, not tomorrow. They will freeze your bank account.

I woke up one morning and went to the bank, and discovered that the IRS took $7,000 of my money. They just took it and the bank did not notify me. They just let them have my money. I was like, "Don't I get a notice or anything?" They sent a notice, but I don't live there anymore. Why do we fill out those cards to change your address at the post office anyway? The IRS is a leech. They take your money, and what do they do with it? They spend $400 on a bucket, $700 on a hammer, and I sit there and look at TV and I can't help but think that's *my* money. **They just gave my money to the Bosnians.** No one in my family is a Serb, a Bosnian, or a Russian. Those are not my people. Why are you sending my money to these people? They took my money, they took Dre's money, and they gave us a $13 refund.

They don't care if you've got a bill to pay, they take your money. The more money you make, the more you have to give to the government. You sit there and wonder, "Why am I giving this money to the government while they sit there and cut educational programs and the things people need in the 'hood?"

ED'S IN THE MUSIC BUSINESS

EXCERPT OF A HOT 97 INTERVIEW WITH BARRY WHITE

ED: Joinin' us right now in the Hot 97 studio is the man. He's a living legend, he is the Maestro of all time. Mr. Barry White is in the house with us.

BARRY: Thank you, guys.

ED: And the voice is just still incredible. You got a brand-new album out in the stores right now, *The Icon Is Love*. Fabulous album. I read somewhere where you said in an interview that the problem now is that the young guys out there, the young people that's makin' music today, don't know how to write songs.

Barry White with the Hot 97 Morning Show gang.

What did you mean by that?

BARRY: Ah, I don't think I said exactly that. I said some of them . . . not all. We have our young masters today who know how to write songs very well. I don't think a lot of people, young people, take music serious enough.

ED: I agree.

BARRY: And that's gonna cause them to . . . break their hearts later down the road. Let me put it to you that way. Music is something that should be taken very, very serious. The only way that you can have longevity with music, you must take it serious.

ED: No question.

I agree with Barry there. We have to take our music more seriously today. My goal with my label is to develop and stand behind talent. If Relativity Records does not allow me to do that, then I will take my label and do it somewhere else.

I don't think there's any development of talent anymore. Nobody cares about talent anymore. I think it's gonna be so difficult for me because my whole concept and direction of where I want to go as a businessman with my record label is so different from the popular stuff now. I would never let an artist that I'm dealing with touch a cover tune unless they added something spectacular to a tune that was done for them. I want music to come back. I want the young people that's comin' up now to have somebody they can look back to and say, "God, this was an innovator." I just want talented people to have their chance. Let's stop worrying if a person looks hard or are they good-looking. If a person can blow, what difference does that make? I think image has superseded real talent. Some R&B groups are totally wack. I don't mean to trash them. I like them as people, but people get the wrong idea. When I meet somebody and I like them as a person, it doesn't mean I'm gonna agree with their music and everything they do. Dionne Farris said it best in *Vibe*. She said some of these girls have potential, but if they took singing lessons they'd be a lot better. You have to hone and practice your craft. It shouldn't be all about a look. Regardless of what you may think of their image, the R&B group Jodeci is still very capable of giving you that down-home feeling because of K-Ci and Jo-Jo's vocal abilities. They're very much capable of giving you that good old grit-blowing.

I tell my friend LeLe from SWV you gotta reach for it this time. Every album you do should get better. If you're not getting better, you're wasting your time. You gotta let the audience grow with you. As Sprite so well put it, "Image is nothing, thirst is everything." You gotta be thirsty and hungry, and you gotta be a singer. If you look at TLC, they've grown from the bubblegum image to an "I'm coming into my sexuality, I'm feminine, I'm a woman—hear me roar"–type of thing. It's cool. If you want to be the next Whitney, Mariah, Anita, or Sade, you gotta reach. It's not enough to say Mary J. Blige sold two million, so I wanna do two and a half million, or TLC sold six million, so we wanna do six million. You're supposed to be like, "I want to do eight million or twelve million." You can't stay in a box.

I love the music industry and entertainment field so much. I love to see new people get put on and do their thing. But, man, these record companies really don't care. It's about the almighty dollar. I wanna see when these people go in here and try to make an example out of Snoop and find him guilty of conspiracy to murder and give him fifteen years in the pen, I wanna see how many people are still on his jock then. It's gonna be very interesting to see who pays visits. Ain't no fans runnin' up to see Tupac. Mike Tyson is the only one I know that got visits all the time. I'm not sayin' any one of them is guilty. All I'm sayin' is that there's no loyalty, no support.

If people can't hear where I'm comin' from, even with the groups I'm shopping, then I stop talking. If you don't hear it, I don't hit you in the head about it. I say thank you very much and then go somewhere else with it.

HOBNOBBING WITH THE GOOBER SMOOCHERS

YOU must be scratching your head right about now wondering, *What in the hell is a goober smoocher and on top of that why would anyone want to hobnob with one?* Well, we'll give it to you straight: A goober smoocher is a rich and powerful person. Sometimes a celebrity, sometimes not, but read on and we think you'll get the idea.

THE SPECIAL SAUCE

OUR version of an *Enquirer*-type magazine would be called *The Special Sauce*. We'd have articles that gave our readers the real and sometimes not-so-real stories about the dynasties, couples, and conspiracies that make it dynamite. Here are some of our best stories.

What do you want from Santa, little boy?

ED ON THE JACKSON DYNASTY

Just like Michael Jackson and his crazy shit. "Kick me, kike me, don'tcha Black or white me." What does he mean? Don'tcha Black or white me? You are Black, Mike! You are gonna be Black until the day you die. Am I Black or white? He asked this question in his song? You don't know? You having a problem figuring out what you are? I don't think Michael Jackson thinks he's a color, and that's why he did that to himself. Now he's not a color. He probably doesn't put down a nationality. Like if he filled out a job application, he would just put down "pale." I think something is deeply, psychologically wrong.

think he's a hell of an entertainer. I don't take nothing away from him. I think what he does onstage with a song is incredible. I think something got mixed up in his coming up. I don't buy that whole vitiligo thing because I've seen people with vitiligo. Actually I know a girl that has vitiligo, and you never actually just turn white. Never. I don't care what the doctors say, you don't ever just turn white. You spot and there's treatments that the doctors can give you. Michael is whiter than his wife. How do you become whiter than a white person? **He's whiter than a white woman**. He's white! He looks white, and he no longer looks like a man. He looks like something in between a man and a woman, and I don't really think that's what he set out to do when he started with his nose surgery. The last time Michael was Black was *Thriller*. I was watching MTV. He took over MTV for the whole weekend and they showed the whole *Thriller* thing. He was Black then, and I was like, "Damn, Mike was Black; he had color." There were no signs of vitiligo then. Then they showed *Bad* and he got lighter. Then they showed "Remember the Time," and he got lighter, and then they showed "Scream," with him and Janet, and he's like white. I want to know what is the process. It must be a painful process that you have to go through to go from Black to white. Do they get a potato peeler like my mother used to have and soak them until your skin is loose? And just peel it off? What is that chemical peel? He's lighter than an albino. I got two albinos that I know that live in Cambria Heights. They're albino brothers and Michael Jackson is lighter than them. And albinos are the lightest people I've ever seen in my life. My God, **he's whiter than an albino!**

Now he's married to a white woman. Now don't get me wrong. Half of me says, "To each his own"; half of Ed says, "If you love her, love is blind," it doesn't matter if she's white or you're Black. Then the other half of me says, "That's a white woman. You have no business with a white woman." It's the whitest white woman in the world. It's Elvis Presley's daughter. Lisa Marie probably never had a Black friend in her whole entire life and probably knows absolutely nothing about Black people. Mike married her. A white woman. He couldn't go find a sister? It shows what he married. He doesn't like being Black and he'll sit up there in interviews with Oprah and Diane Sawyer, and claim "I'm proud to be Black. I don't hate myself. I love what I am." But first you turned yourself into a white person and then you turned around and married a white person. So you're not proud of what you are. You don't love your people. Most of the people that Michael Jackson ever said he loved the most in his life are white people. It's never a Black person. Even the little boy that he was accused of molesting and having sex with was a little white kid. You never see a little Black kid around Michael Jackson, except when he used to have Webster around him. I guess Webster and Michael were both loners.

I don't know, but I think it's something from growing up and being famous since you were five years old. It's psychological. After they put out that first record there was nowhere he could go in the country and then, eventually, the world, without people being on him. And since he was the lead singer and they pursued him more than anyone else, I guess it had an adverse effect on him. But look at Tito. Tito's straight, Tito never had a nose job. He's fat, he's got an afro. He plays the damn guitar. I love Tito. **Tito's my favorite Jackson of all time.**

Jermaine's out of his mind. I read in the news that Jermaine married Randy's woman or ex-woman— the woman that Randy's got two kids with. Jermaine hooked up with her and married her and didn't tell Randy. Randy beats the hell out of his wife. Marlon's just doing his thing. Tito's ex-wife, DeeDee, was found dead in a swimming pool somewhere. Joe Jackson looks like the Tasmanian devil. Katherine sits around and doesn't say anything.

Janet Jackson is dynamite, but she does what she has to do. She does all the little pull this out, tuck this under there, and then people go, **"Janet Jackson is so beautiful!" She paid for it!** If I had that much money I'd be beautiful too. I'd just get this moved and tuck the ass here and move my booty to the side over here and lift that! I have to give it to her, though, she works what she paid for out every day so it looks dynamite! But hell yeah, you can pay for beauty.

La Toya, oh God! La Toya is a stripper. She's out there in Europe making people pay $50 to see her.

Look, La Toya has no talent, none! Who is the only other Jackson who is a sane one? Besides Tito, it's Rebbie. La Toya is out of her freakin' mind. "Oh, Joe molested me." La Toya, come on. Your tits are fake, your nose is fake, and I've never seen you and Michael Jackson at the same time. There is no La Toya; she is Mike in a wig and stick-on breasts. That's Mike. **Mike and La Toya is the same thing.** You never see them together (except USA for Africa). I used to think Janet and Mike were the same until they showed up together.

I hear Mike uses doubles. I don't know how true that is, but I hear he has guys who live with him who look exactly like him. They work for him and they've had all the surgeries he's had. This kid on Long Island, Fame Jackson, he's a Michael Jackson impersonator, so I believe that it's possible. The guy will go one way and everybody will follow him, and Mike will go the other way, and he dances like him but he doesn't say anything. He'll just wave his hand. If you put Fame in a car with a police escort and Fame just waved, you wouldn't know it wasn't Michael. I guess when you get that much money, you get bored, and after the animals and the big amusement park and having $300 million, what is there left to do but claim yourself as the king of every goddamn thing. I'm the King of Pop. I married the King of Rock's daughter and I'm trying to have a little whatever. It was a marriage of convenience, and now, as you know, Lisa Marie doesn't think it's convenient anymore.

I never did believe that Michael Jackson was a pedophile. But I think Michael shouldn't have put himself in that position. I think Mike has to realize what came to him was a form of racism. They just went after Michael Jackson because he's a Black man. He set himself up by having those kids around him all the time and it was just to get some money. I think that's a terrible thing to put your kids through—making your kid a victim or having your kid say something just to get some money.

MIKE, MIKE, AND MIKE

It was the decade of Mikes. The last five years have been Kill the Mikes. Let's get rid of all three top Michaels in this world: Michael Jackson, Michael Jordan, and Mike Tyson. So they went after Mike Tyson, they got him. They went after Michael Jordan, they couldn't get him. But he said, "I've had enough. I'm tired of all of y'all being in my business. I'll go play baseball." And then they went after Michael Jackson. I seriously do believe that it was a conspiracy to get all the Mikes because when you are a Black man and get too big, they start looking for a reason to bring you down.

MIKE TYSON AND THE GREAT ADVENTURES

We got one, he set himself up. Desiree Washington needs her ass whipped for bringing that man down like that. She needs 1-800-ASS-WHIPPIN' like everybody else. That's a shame, she said, "I felt so dirty and degraded. It's not about the money." Then she turned around and settled out of court for an undisclosed amount of money. Someone told me she told her friends at the beauty pageant, "He's not that good-looking, but he's got money." So it's been about the money. So Mike Tyson sets himself up and in Indiana. Oh my God, one of the worst places in the world for a Black man to do anything (Indiana or Denver). Mike Tyson is one of my favorite celebrities of all time because I hung out with Mike and Mike is a lot of fun.

I don't think it was right, because Mike Tyson got railroaded into a conviction that never should have happened. Yeah, he's a role model. But convicted by what? Mike Tyson wasn't convicted by a jury of his own peers. Mike Tyson was convicted in Indiana, one of the most racist states in the country. Give me a break, convicted of what? The point is they keep asking if he's going to say he's sorry and he keeps going, "Sorry for what? I never did anything." There's plenty of Black men that go to prison for stuff they didn't do. If I knew in my heart that I didn't rape that woman, I don't give a damn if they gave me fifteen years, I would never apologize. Never.

Robin Givens was after the money. Robin is a conniving, sneaky, low-down snake-in-the-grass bitch. Robin Givens was after Mike Tyson for his money, that's it. Robin Givens's mother used to send her pictures out to all the bachelor guys and the top entertainment bachelor guys like Eddie Murphy. I never thought that she was really that attractive. The only time I thought Robin Givens really kind of looked good was in the movie *A Rage in Harlem.* That's the only time I thought she looked good. Other than that, she's a little bitch. I didn't think she was all that dynamite. I think Mike Tyson was just vulnerable. She was kind of like a dream girl for him. He was into her and she hurt his feelings. She dissed him hard. Tyson's limo driver wrote it in his book, *The Inside Ring.* That book is really kind of interesting, to know what kind of stuff she did to him.

Tyson's my man, though. We've done a few things together. Me and Tyson went to the Q Club one night and they wouldn't let us in because we had on sneakers and it was a shoe night. The Q Club is a notorious reggae club in Queens. They don't give a damn who you are. If you don't have on the proper attire, they will not let you in. Mike Tyson was the undisputed heavyweight champion at the time, and they wouldn't let him or me or the entire entourage in 'cause we had on sneakers. Tyson had on a $30,000 mink jacket, a Fila suit, and a skully, and they still wouldn't let him in. Some girl said, "You need to learn how to dress when you go out." Mike went off. He said, "You see this, Ed? See how they treat me!" Then he hit me on the shoulder and almost knocked me in the street. That's my man Mike.

He punched me a second time, as a matter of fact, the same day Dre broke his fence. Oh, that's on film. That has been documented. Dre and I were doing a segment and Mike and I got into this Brooklyn vs. Queens thing. So Dre asks Mike what it is that gave him that killer instinct. What is it that made him so much tougher than every other heavyweight. Mike goes, "Well, Dre, as you know, I'm from Brooklyn. I grew up in Bedford-Stuyvesant, and you know niggas is hard out there. We don't fuck around, man. We

knock a nigga out. I'm from Brooklyn, you know." I said, "Man, this Brooklyn crap. I'm from Queens and I

didn't come out here to hear that old Brooklyn garbage." So they had me do a stay-tuned. I'm in front of

Dre and Mike. Dre is talking to Mike and I go, "Mike Tyson is getting ready to fight Razor Ruddock and

we're here at *Yo! MTV Raps,* stay tuned. Don't go nowhere, I don't care what Mike says, no Brooklyn punk ever did nothin' to a brotha from Queens and we'll—" And Mike ran up behind me and said, "Oh, Ed, you think you're funny?" *BUYAKA!* right in the side and everything just left. You see me on the screen and I just drop. Out. Mike doesn't understand how strong he is. He hit me and it was over, and he goes, "So now you're gonna sue me, Ed? Oh shit, Ed Lover's gonna sue me." I'm just like, Take me in the house 'cause I want to sit down for an hour. You can't say you're going to sue because you're trying to find your air. He's got to be one of my favorite celebrities.

ON THE COURT WITH MICHAEL JORDAN

Michael Jordan's father was brutally murdered. God rest his father's soul. But what's the first thing that was said? "Oh, it could have been because of one of his gambling debts." Let's bring another Black man down, why don't we. How much money does Michael Jordan make? He makes approximately $35 million a year. What gambling debts could the man have made that he couldn't pay for? Then he returned to basketball and people started to say, "He needs the money for his gambling debts." I know some of Michael's friends and he's a gambler at heart. He is an athlete and he likes to make small bets on anything from nine-hole to who goes under par in golf. But as far as getting into the millions and millions of dollars—NO! He makes approximately $32 million in endorsements alone. That's why he can afford to take the cut in pay so that the Bulls can acquire a better team so they can win world championships.

Michael Jordan is the best. Michael Jordan is a nice guy all around. The day he came back to basketball the Bulls were playing the Knicks. I was working on the NBA Slammin' Jam wrap-up for MTV and they came out. They were doing the layup line and I was on the floor, and you know when you haven't seen somebody for a long time. Well, I was thinking, He's not going to remember me; he probably meets so many people. And then he goes around and lays it up and he comes around and we catch eyes. He stops and goes, "Ed, what's happening." He comes over, says hi, and then he went back and did his thing. He's the best.

Me and Mike gigged on Dominique Wilkins's one time at Charlotte (at the all-star game, I went down there). Dominique just thought he was so much of a ladies' man. But me and Jordan were talking because I know Adolf, who's been Jordan's best friend since high school. He finally introduced us and we were talking. It's like whenever Michael Jordan is in a room, the whole room shifts in his direction, and if he moves, the room shifts the other way. It's weird. It's like being around Shaq. It's the same thing, the room just shifts. It's just weird.

DENNIS RODMAN AND MADONNA

I think Dennis Rodman is out of his freakin' mind to even consider getting down with Madonna. Madonna will sleep with anybody. I heard even Vanilla Ice slept with Madonna. Anybody can sleep with Madonna. All you got to do is be famous, buck wild, an' don't give a fuck and you can sleep with Madonna. But let me tell you somethin', you betta know how to fuck or else you're outta there! Madonna could be naked in my bed, I wouldn't touch Madonna. I would really have to tell her to get up and go home. Get her out of here.

THE O.J. SIMPSON FLEA CIRCUS

EXCERPT OF A HOT 97 INTERVIEW WITH DICK GREGORY

ED: Dick, did you know O.J. personally?

DICK: No, I did not know him personally, but I know more about him watching this trial. The trial confused me so bad one day I shut it off and I thought I did it.

DRE: What is your whole take on the O.J. situation and the mishap with the police?

DICK: O.J. is the one who flips me out. He sits there and he's writing and writing and he is the only one who does not go to the sidebar and writes and writes.

ED: That's the book.

DICK: He gives it to Shapiro . . .

ED: He gives it to Shapiro, and Shapiro runs it over to his book publisher.

DICK: O.J. can't write. He is a dumb student, good athlete. Shapiro probably told him to write ten thousand times, "I will never have a white lady again. I will never have a white lady again."

I guess even us Black people don't care if O.J. is guilty or not. I don't think the majority of Black people want to see him locked up. That trial has been a mistrial since day one. Judge Lance Ito needed to be thrown off the seat since day one. There's too much little stupid, technical evidence that has nothing to do with the trial, like Faye Resnick and Kato "the Moocher" Kaelin. That's another ass whippin' I would like to give out. You stayed at this man's house, you lived off this man and his wife. You did nothing for him and now you're running around trying to become a celebrity off his misery.

O.J. was another one who set himself up. I can't feel sorry for O.J. because O.J. never wanted to be down with Black people. O.J. was never there for Black folks. He left his Black wife for a white woman. I met his daughter Arnelle and she is cool. She's very close to her mother. She loves her father because that's her father. But the **Juice never wanted to be Black.** Everybody has a right to their own personal opinion. When the O.J. verdict came in, I sat in my car and listened to it on the radio. All by myself. I just sat there and listened to the foreperson say, "Not guilty. Not guilty." I was so happy, I just cried. You see, to many Black people O.J. has become a symbol of justice. Even though we know how bad he wanted to be a part of white society, we still feel like he was and is one of us. We all know through various incidents that the Los Angeles Police Department has been proven to be one of the most racist police departments in the country. Mark Fuhrman proved that! The department knew he was racist and they still left him on the job. A lot of us feel that O.J.'s acquittal is payback for the "not guilty" verdicts in the first Rodney King trial, the light sentences given to the killers of Yusef Hawkins, Medgar Evers, the Scottsboro Boys, et cetera. I could go on and on.

Congratulations, O.J. Now go home and take care of your children and live your life.

WHITNEY HOUSTON AND BOBBY BROWN

I think all the big-society women—the rich, powerful women—need a buck-wild man at times. See, that's why Whitney's straight, because Bobby can get buck wild. That's what she likes. She was dating Randall Cunningham and Eddie Murphy. Eddie was rich, he was making the dough. So his style changed 'cause he didn't want them to have nothin' to say about him. When Whitney got with Bobby Brown, Bobby tore her to shreds. Bobby's a buck-wild nigga from Boston, and he got at Whitney and rocked her world. They're in love and it shows. Bobby's satisfying her at every opportunity. He's tearing her up. He's ill, I love him.

OPRAH AND STEDMAN

I like Oprah. I think Oprah needs a good man. Stedman stepped on my foot at the Essence Awards, and I had to tell him to raise up off my shit. I mean, he was standing there talking to David Dinkins on my foot. Now I'm sitting in the aisle seat, Sted is standing on my alligators. "Money, you're on my foot." And he's talkin'. "Brotha, you are on my foot." He was still talking, and I was like *"Stedman!"* And he turned around and said, "Sorry." I'm like, "Get off my foot, Money. I ought to charge Oprah for you standing on my foot." Oprah's fine! Hey Oprah, if ya ever get sick of that foot-steppin'-on Stedman, give me a call. I'm diggin' your style, peachie.

TO BE PERFECTLY FRANK . . .

To be perfectly frank, there are a lot of stars out there that we've met over the years or just observed and they deserve a shout-out.

ED'S STAR WATCH

WOODY ALLEN

I avoid Woody Allen's stuff like the plague. I don't see how he can have no Black people in his films. Besides that, he slept with his daughter, adopted or not. I saw Woody Allen once at a Knicks game and I wanted to knock his teeth out. But I didn't want it to be in the papers. Headline: **Ed Lover knocks out Woody Allen**

MEL GIBSON

Mel was cool. Mel did *Yo! MTV Raps* for us on the spur of the moment when he was in a rush to somewhere else. We improvised the whole thing.

HUGH GRANT

Hugh did a great publicity blitz for the opening of his latest movie, *Nine Months*. What genius—being caught in a drop top, ass naked behind a 7-Eleven with a prostitute. What's the matter, Hugh? Your publicist went on vacation, so you decided to step in. Well, you stepped in it all right!

SYLVESTER STALLONE

Sylvester Stallone wasn't what I expected at all. He's short. In all his movies they make him look bigger than life. I was kind of disappointed when I had to look down at him. He's like 5'5". They weren't lying when they say the camera adds five to ten pounds, 'cause in Sly's case it adds five to ten inches.

JEAN-CLAUDE VAN DAMME

Jean-Claude Van Damme was funny. Dre and I had him on the show and we asked if there was any one person he could work with who would it be, and he looked directly into the camera with the most sincerity he could muster and said, "My beautiful wife, because I love her so much." So we're shooting all day, and then we had to do pickup shots and everything. So then we didn't get off 'til like one, two o'clock in the morning. Me and Dre are walking in the parking lot, getting ready to go back to the hotel, and it's damn near empty. Except there's this car and Jean-Claude Van is in it with some young woman, his head thrown back in ecstacy. I'm not saying what she was doing but she wasn't fixing his zipper. Thank you, Jean-Claude. Then, a few weeks later, he's breaking up with his wife.

ROSEANNE

Roseanne's dynamite. We expected her to be a bitch, but she was cool. I like Tom Arnold. I thought he was so funny. That's why in *True Lies* he did so well. I think they helped each other. It was very much a hand-in-hand situation. I like people who are straight up. And, Roseanne, she's straight up. You couldn't even tell at the time that Roseanne had millions and millions of dollars. She didn't treat us like snooty.

LEONA HELMSLEY

One time I was a security guard, and she was standing by the door at the Helmsley. I came across the street and she was just standing there talking to somebody. I guess every Black man Leona Helmsley sees has to work for her. She just came out of the door and dropped her bags and looked at me and asked if I was going to get her bags. I was like, "Hell, no! I don't work here. Get your own damn bags." Needless to say, I was real happy to see her go to prison.

BRUCE WILLIS

I did one thing with Bruce Willis. I had heard he didn't want to work with me because I was hosting *Yo! MTV Raps*. We were all right because we both understood each other. I did something with him for Planet Hollywood. I was interviewing him and I said, "I heard you hate rap music." He said, "Yeah, I can't stand it." I said, "Well, I hate that harmonica bullshit you be playing, too. So now we understand each other, so let's get the interview going on." He was cool after that.

PAT RILEY

Pat Riley is a good coach and I think the Knicks should've let him have a little more say-so on who gets put on the team. They should've let him be general manager because he did wonders with the Knicks. I think Pat Riley needs to run a team, the whole team. He should make trading and acquisition decisions. I kind of dig Pat Riley, slick hair and all.

GILBERT GOTTFRIED

☆✄—!!! (bleep) ☆ (bleep)!!! ☆

I love Gilbert Gottfried. When he's on camera, he just starts with all that stuff that he does. Gilbert and I have an ongoing joke every Spring Break because he used to be there every year. So we had an ongoing joke from year to year that he would see me and he would just start cursing.

He would walk around going, "Shit, fuck, damn, bitch, motherfucker, dick, cock . . ." and I would sit there and laugh at him. Then I wouldn't see him for the whole year and as soon as he'd see me at Spring Break, he'd start, "shit, bitch, cunt . . ." Gilbert is a great guy.

PAULY SHORE

Pauly Shore's got a thing. I respect his thing, his style. I saw his standup routine when he had the HBO special and I didn't think he was that funny because his humor doesn't appeal to me. I think Pauly's doing it because he knows who he's playing to and who it appeals to. I respect him, but do I think he's a great comedian? No, I don't.

MARTIN LAWRENCE

I think Martin Lawrence has changed from what he used to be to what he is now. I think you have to change toward people and you have to become more guarded, and I can't blame him for that. But he didn't have to change toward me. His personality changed. He was like the kind of guy who would see you and he would embrace you and laugh and box with you. Then it became like a brush-off. I've stood there in a room with me, him, Derrick Coleman, and Todd 1, and all of us watching him cry because he never had friends like us before. *Crying.* I couldn't tell you what goes through Martin's head. But I do feel that he's changed toward some of us that love him.

DRE'S TALKIN' TRASH

I have a few words to say about some of these talk show hosts. Not only are they taking over the channels, it seems like you can turn the channel and see the same couple on two different shows at the same time talking about how the husband cheated with his wife's sister's mother-in-law in a nursing home only to find out he was her illegitimate love child. Here's my take on the most popular ones out there.

I forgot my shinguards when I was on <u>Geraldo.</u>

GERALDO

I think Geraldo gets a bad rap, but I also think Geraldo wants that rep because that's his thing. He's a talk show sploitationist. He basically exploits everything he has on his talk show. He had the highest ratings until the last two minutes when he popped the Al Capone vaults open. He should have had a guy in there dressed up like Al Capone going, "Gee, thanks, man." Geraldo's all right with me. He gives me and Ed a lot of exposure and a lot of work. He's always been respectful. He's not one of those guys who goes, "I've seen you and I enjoy your work," and you know he's never seen you before a day in his life. Geraldo is always cool like that.

RICKI LAKE

I think Ricki Lake is a male basher. I think Ricki Lake is a hype. She lost her weight for the hype. She got a talk show for the hype, and the people she puts on are hype. The last time we did Ricki Lake, I told Ed I didn't want to do it anymore. It's just too much. It's a set-up show. When they're not rolling, they're like, "Go, go get at each other some more." They're not trying to solve problems. They're trying to create problems for ratings. That's ridiculous, just like all of a sudden getting arrested for protesting the sale of animal fur. Please, honey, you're a bit much.

JENNY JONES

Jenny Jones is becoming too far-out for the sake of the ratings. I don't think that guy that was on her show had the right to kill the other guy. But there are a lot of men out there who don't like being on TV and having a homosexual come and display his affection for you on national television. I think Jenny Jones should have told him that it was another man that was diggin' him. She just told him that he had a secret admirer. She didn't know what his reaction would be, and he didn't think it was dynamite.

RICHARD BEY

Richard's wild and crazy, but at least you know where he's coming from. He doesn't try to hide behind the guise of helping the guest. He just gets right to the point with the mudslinging, insult making, and fighting. He never pretends to be something he's not as far as the format of his show. I respect him for that.

A tender moment with Richard Bey.

OPRAH

I think she's about the only one out of the bunch that has kept the integrity when it comes to talk shows. She deals with topics that reach and touch millions of people every day. She has a large female audience that she caters to, but I kinda get into it. It really makes me think. I wish she had more Black guests on her show, but that's another section altogether.

IN THE HOUSE

IT took us a while to realize that we were considered celebrities. There were definite indicators, like the time . . .

There was this major concert thing that Dre and I had to do with N.W.A. Joe Louis Arena was packed to the rafters in Detroit and the guy was having trouble with N.W.A. They wasn't supposed to do "Fuck tha Police," but they did the song anyway. I'm standing there on the side and like a couple of people that saw me, they were waving. Then one of the cops threw an M-80 on the stage and N.W.A thought the cops were shooting at them. So they dropped everything and they ran offstage to their dressing rooms. Darryl Brooks, who was the promoter, promised that he would pay me and Dre $5,000 apiece to go onstage to calm the audience down. When me and Dre walked out on that stage and everybody stood up and started clapping and screaming, right at that moment when I stepped out, I said to myself, **"Damn, I'm famous."** That's when I knew it, right then. I think we wasn't on MTV no more than a year. As a matter of fact, I think that was our first major trip outside the city. I knew a lot of people in N.Y. watched it, but I knew a lot of people didn't have cable in '89.

ED'S DEALINGS WITH STARDOM

BEING a celebrity has its good points and its bad points. The good points of being a celebrity are that you can pretty much get into any damn club anytime you want to. No matter what they say about the guest list, you're in. And no matter how much you're drinking, you ain't gotta pay for nothing. You get a lot of clothes, a lot of sneakers, a lot of shit. You get to travel a lot and meet the people you've admired your whole life. You get to finally meet them and they know you and respect what you do. You get to go to exclusive parties, but after you've done that about one hundred times, there ain't nothin' left to that. The chicks are great.

The down part of being a celebrity is that people feel they can say anything. "Ed, what you doing in that car? Where's your car at? **Goddamn, you should at least have a Lamborghini or something** all that damn money you got. Who dat? Where you live at? What you doing here? Where's Dre? I love y'all motherfuckers. Buy me a drink." That's the down part. No privacy!!! The kids in my building bring their friends over and knock on my apartment door. People think that you're rich, and your Uncle Atlas calls at three in the morning and tells you about a cockamamie idea to start some little business and asks you for $50,000. Then he'll get mad at you when you tell him you don't have it. When you go out with your friends, y'all can eat up $700 worth of stuff and everybody waits for you to pull out your wallet. These are the same people you grew up with.

Sometimes I really want to be left alone. I don't mind the "hi"s and "how are you doing, Ed?" But the snide comments like I owe you something just because you listen to me is the thing that bothers me. If I'm not entertaining you, then you wouldn't listen to me.

"Keepin' it real" is a bullshit cop-out. What is "keepin' it real"? Keepin' it real is whatever is real to you. I love my mother, so I'm keepin' it real. I take care of my kids; that's keepin' it real. I'm not keepin' it real because I don't smoke blunts? Smokin' blunts doesn't mean you're keepin' it real. I hear it every day, "Keep it real, Ed." My reality of keepin' it real is to do as much as I can to further my career and to put other people on if they're talented enough and deserve it (not because they come and ask me to). I've had people try to use their beauty to try and influence me to do something for them. I can spot that a million miles away. I can tell when I get a phone call that you're not just trying to see how I'm doing, because then you get around to asking me for tickets to some event. That's really what the phone call was about in the first place. Why didn't you just come out and ask me? Don't play yourself like, "Yeah Ed, what's happening? Whatcha doing? . . . You think you can get any extra tickets?" That's what this call is about. I would prefer if you call and say, "Yo, Ed, this is so-and-so. I was wondering if you could help me. I'm trying to get concert tickets." I would prefer you come straight at me. A lot of times I've regretted giving someone my number. But I just can't say no. How many times has someone asked you for your number and you've said no?

DRE'S DEALINGS WITH STARDOM

I always knew what I wanted to do since I was fourteen years old. I knew! There was no alternative. The alternative was success. If it was going to be failure, you just rubbed off your knees.

You do things to become successful and I don't think I am successful yet. I think I'm growing and learning what success is about and how to become successful. But I don't feel I am successful right now. I think I am getting to that stage. I don't think success is measured in dollars and cents. I think success is measured in action and what you do with what you have. Success radiates success.

Success is based upon your actions and what you do when you are given certain things. When I say "given certain things," I mean given opportunity.

There's a lot of people out there who have a lot of money who aren't successful. "First you get the money. Then you get the women. Then you get the power," to quote Scarface.

The down part of being a celebrity is that people feel they can say anything they want to say to you. I'll give you a good example of that. On the Fourth of July, I'm at Pergament. I'm purchasing a few briquettes and a few other things for my BBQ. I'm standing on the line and a woman walks up to me. Not may I, or can I, she says, "Autograph this for me now. You ain't doing nothin'. I listen every day. Remember when you and Ed were talking . . ." She just rambled on. I told her that we're on every day, that Ed and I do a lot of shows, and that sometimes I just don't remember. **So I took the paper and I signed it "Joe E. Nobody."** I folded it up and gave it to her and said thanks. She took it and didn't even open it to see if I wrote my name or not.

Better yet, one o'clock in the morning the bell rings. I look out the window. I don't see nothing. I don't hear a car pull up, so I go downstairs. I open the door and it's four kids. "Hi, I was wondering, well, my friend and I . . ." I did a George Jefferson—I slammed the door. It was one in the morning, for God's sake! Where are your parents??!! Not at one in the morning. Not when I'm at the urinal in Giant Stadium. Don't ask me for an autograph when I'm taking a piss. I'm normally very cordial when people come up to me in a nice way and ask for an autograph, but some people can be just downright rude!

The thing that bugs me the most is when they say something about me, Doctor Dre, doing something. They'll print a picture of Dr. Dre from the West Coast because they don't do their research. They don't know us like we know them. I don't get Steven Tyler mixed up with anybody else from Aerosmith. I know who they're talking about. Or the Mark Walberg with the talk show mixed up with the Mark Wahlberg of Marky Mark and the Funky Bunch of Calvin Klein underwear fame of course except Marky Mark's own mother!

THIS section represents some of our other philosophies about life. You bought the damn book and now you're about to hear how we feel about everything from a Black man's point of view. Everything you need to know is in this section, so get your highlighters ready and let's get busy!

1-800-ASS-WHIPPIN'

Kids don't have any discipline today. That's why we need 1-800-ASS-WHIPPIN'. Call me and Dre and we'll come to your house and whip your kids' asses. You can't beat your kids today because of BCW. They even have a number for kids to call: 1-800-HE-HURTME and they'll come and take your kids away from you. That's the problem. It wasn't like that when we were growing up. Our mothers would go outside, pick up a tree, bring it in and pick a selected switch off of that tree, and then treat it like a samurai sword. She'd soak it in warm water for half an hour, tie an extension cord around it, and whip your ass. But nowadays they don't do that. Kids today carry guns, smoke blunts, and hang out all night, and it's all because they're not being disciplined.

The things we had when we grew up, kids don't have now. We always had something constructive to do and our parents spent valuable time with us. They taught us and guided us. Children have no guidance today. Back when we were little, we used to get ass whippin's. I mean those real "you fucked up" ass whippin's.

TV today is too violent and sexual. It used to be that if anything sexual came on TV, it was shown after ten o'clock at night. But nowadays it's not like that. The cartoons they show today are too violent, the soap operas are too sexual, and the talk shows are ridiculous.

And now Showbiz (from Showbiz and AG), he's not that famous, but we know him in the hip-hop community; they're saying he killed somebody. Slick Rick is in jail. And now with Tupac and Snoop, they're living their records. It's ironic, but if you take each rapper's life, it seems to copy his raps—like Tupac in "Dear Mama" mentions "hugging on my mama from a jail cell. Will I live to see nineteen or end up in the penitentiary?" or Snoop writes, "Murder was the case that they gave me." No, murder is the case that they're slapping you with. And Slick Rick's "Children's Story" record is basically the same thing that happened to him. They have to understand that this is business. We think they are a product of their environment. They're a bunch of young guys who made it rich and never had no money before. So of course they're not going to know how to act. You can't expect a little boy to act like a man regardless of how much money you put in his pocket. It all comes rushing at you at one time. It's not funny. We think they have to be on guard because the media surely is on point.

We'll go around to schools and talk to kids about growing up. We'll let them know that there's people out there they can come to and talk to when they get into problem situations, because they're making life-altering decisions at such young ages without thinking about the long term. We wanna do that even if we have to bring a musical act with us. That's gonna be so hard to find. Rosie Perez took Ed to Thomas

Jefferson High School and they spoke and it was cool. We think it would be cool if we get the teachers and everybody involved with it. We're trying to get Hot 97 in the game. We can give the kids fat packs and Hot 97 T-shirts and whatever new tape is out. We're trying to get Jodeci to maybe come along and do a show. But we have to moderate what these performers do because you can't get up there in an auditorium in front of these kids taking your shirt off and grinding your pelvic bone. Naughty by Nature is a group that we'd ask to go with us and perform one of their songs. You can't take Mobb Deep, 'cause they gotta be cursing and it's all about blunts.

Some rappers are so scared to take that tough-guy image and put it aside, and even if they did, they lack basic communication skills. I've spoken to Andre Harrell and Andre said when Mary J. Blige comes off tour, I'll try to get Mary to do one or two things with you. I'm like, I don't want Mary to just sing. I want Mary to speak 'cause Mary came from the trenches and she's a success story. She's an inspiration. We have to get to the principals and let the principals lay it on them like they know it.

Don't get us wrong. We're not saying give the kids a beat-down every day. Talk to your kids every day about real-life issues. Prepare them for the future, and you won't need to call 1-800-ASS-WHIPPIN'. We have to take responsibility for all the children—not just our own. But remember, just in case you get in a jam, you can call us and we'll come to your house and whip your kid's ass. Remember our song (sung to the melody of "Ghostbusters"):

When your kids are messin' up in school
Who you gonna call?
ASS-WHIPPIN'!
He's smokin' pot in the backyard too;
Who you gonna call?
ASS-WHIPPIN'!
We ain't afraid of your kids!

THIGH-HIGH IN THE BULLSHIT

THERE hasn't been a real Black leader since Malcolm X and Martin Luther King Jr.

If the government doesn't make it easier for people to survive, we're going to lose a whole generation of children. The government has obviously proven to us that no matter who we vote for, they're not going to change things because it doesn't affect them. So they don't care. It's genocide without them even

lifting a finger. All they got to do is make the right moves to push drugs into the community and they make it hard for people to get decent jobs even with a high school diploma. So those people turn to crime to make ends meet. They have no alternative; they have to live. Then you get a few of us that squeak through and say, "Oh, you can't even do it. I did it, it's crazy."

The guy with the hat and the glasses. What's his name? Ken Hamblin! He's the one I'd really like to kick in his freakin' ass. No, this is what I don't understand about Black conservatives. How do they figure that because they squeaked through that everything is cool for everybody else across the board? It's people like Clarence Thomas, Armstrong Williams, C. DeLores Tucker, who we had the displeasure of debating the issue of gangsta rap with several times last year. They think because they got a Ph.D. or because they squeezed through, that the playing field is level for everybody of all races. It's just not like that. They don't understand how lucky they are, and it really bugged me the other day when I read in the newspaper that Clarence Thomas voted directly against affirmative action in a case that went up in the Supreme Court, and he himself has been a product of affirmative action. His whole career is based on affirmative action, and they just don't understand it. But I always see Ken Hamblin on talk shows and he always wears a fedora-type hat. I would really just love to slap him in his fucking mouth just one time. Just like, *BOW!* Wake up! Wake up, **Uncle Tom, where the hell are you at?** I don't get it.

Those are the worst type of Uncle Toms. If I were them and something ever happened—we were to break out into a racial civil war—I'd run! C. DeLores Tucker doesn't get it. No matter how many times we've debated her, she doesn't understand that the point is not the contents of the lyrics when it comes to rap music or gangsta rap. The point is we all have the right to say what we want to say. She had nothing negative to say about Metallica, Aerosmith, Pearl Jam, Soundgarden, and that guy with the pentagram, Megadeth or whatever. She does have an agenda for them also, but now her focus is mainly on rap. See, it's those kinds of Uncle Toms that make it bad for everybody else. They're the ones who go directly after their own people and hurt their own Black people the worst.

The debate with C. DeLores Tucker was via satellite; she was in Washington, D.C., and we were in New York. What we got from listening to her speak is that this woman doesn't have any idea about what goes on in our neighborhoods. She doesn't know what life is like in the projects. You can get a liquor store in any corner of any block in a Black community. But you don't see that many liquor stores in white communities, and if you do see one it doesn't even look like a damn liquor store. It looks like some big winery or some crap like that. She is so far from the life of the average Black person. That's really a shame; she doesn't get it. She doesn't understand our voice. That's no secret. They don't get it. And people like that, they're the ones that hurt my heart 'cause they don't get it. They're so far beyond Black people. They're not even Black anymore.

She doesn't understand that rap is our way of communicating with each other. It gives a person in New York a feel of what life is like in Long Beach, California. So you don't get caught up in that game if you ever go to Long Beach. You would know that there are some crazy niggas out there. So we're not gonna go in there wearing blue because we don't want to get mixed up in that gang thing. That's the only way we really learn about the gangs. In New York we learned 'bout the California gangs when N.W.A came out with their gangsta rap. We learned a lot about you can't wear colors from Ice Cube.

Unless it was what Public Enemy was doing, you know, with Black pride and Black awareness, I think anything they find incompatible for them is considered gangsta rap music. It's hurtful to me because it's Black people attacking Black people. Bob Dole had absolutely no idea what he was talking about until C. DeLores started with this whole thing along with the Reverend Calvin Butts, who Ed spoke to at a Farrakhan rally in New York. Ed had the pleasure of sitting right next to him, and we decided that we'd get together and open up a forum and talk about this thing. **Ed told him how we and a lot of other people in the industry didn't like it when he threw all those CDs in the street and rolled over them with a steamroller.** We could've come together on something more than that. We could have sat down, and he could have said something. We could have talked to each other about it. People have to understand how to correct the problem in the neighbor-hood. Killing the music is not going to kill the drugs and it's not going to make people who shoot people go away. It's not going to do anything. If you can't express it, you suppress it and you make people go ba-nanas. You can't suppress a culture of people that want to hear about one thing.

C. DeLores Tucker has done her thing. She got Senator Bob Dole behind her now. That's exactly what she was waiting for—somebody with power to get her back. I think a lot of white people are not happy with the Republicans they elected. They're beating us down.

They never go after the media, **they don't go after the movies**. How many people has Arnold Schwarzenegger killed per movie? You know Bruce Willis's *Die Hard,* that says it right there, DIE!—*Die Hard; Die Hard 2: Die Harder; Die Hard with a Vengeance.* How many people do they kill every movie?

You can even see it on TV. You can turn on Channel 9 and see somebody shooting at somebody else. But they don't attack these people. They don't have time.

Where does it end? Do you concentrate on this thing and censor gangsta rap and what rappers can say on records? What's next? Do you censor what we can read after that? Do you censor what tapes we can go to the video store and buy? Then you'll say that's not proper, little kids are get-ting their hands on it, so now we've got to

We all remember <u>Pulp Fiction.</u>

censor that. You can't do that anymore. Where does it end? And they're part of the problem; they're not even part of the solution. They're not even trying to be part of the solution. They're not saying, "Well, look, I understand that it's hard coming up through the neighborhood. But if you do this and do that, then you can make it like I made it." Instead they're just saying, "Stop crying! The white man don't owe you nothing." Hell, yes, the white man owes us a whole hell of a lot. We've been through four hundred years of straight bullshit, and it don't make any difference how much money you make. **We still have to drive our cars to work because we would have problems traveling back and forth in the city because we wouldn't be able to catch a cab.** We'd be out there all day trying to get a taxicab. And that's not based on whether or not we work hard, because we do work hard. It's based on the fact that here's two Black men standing there with baseball caps on. The cab driver is thinking, "He might rob me; I'm not gonna pick him up." Are we supposed to start censoring what we wear to simply get around?

We went down to Guantanamo Bay to help the Haitian refugees, which was Luke's thing. He got all the clothes together from out of Miami. Luke rented a plane to take everybody else down there and then it became a Jesse Jackson spectacular with Congressman Rangel. We spent the whole day with Jesse and his daughter. Jesse's daughter chased Ed all day. We got on the plane and I was talking to Jesse, thinking he's a leader. Then Jesse pulls me to the side and says, "Dre, let me ask you something. Why don't we get all these niggas together and throw a big concert for the Rainbow Coalition. You get all the rap niggas together and I'll get all the political niggas together . . . and we'll get all the shit done right." We were surprised because while he came at us like we were his people on the street, just talkin', it also made me realize his perception of me and how he felt that the only way to relate to us was on that level. **We're businessmen who run our own businesses** jointly and separately, and we can speak English on his level, or anyone else's, for that matter. It made me feel real messed up. I hate when brothers do that.

ART PARTIES, POETRY, AND PORNOGRAPHY

SOME people can do anything and still get paid. One motherfucker got a bucket of paint, threw it on canvas, called it abstract, and sold it for $280,000. Andy Warhol painted a big fuckin' can of soup and got paid for it. I don't get it. Motown Records executive Andre Harrell gave an art showing for this artist he discovered. Everybody was in the room—models, actors, singers, executives—and I walked over and said, "What the fuck is this about?" Everybody looked at me like, "You don't feel it, Ed?" "No! The motherfucker took some paint and slapped it up there!" That shit is bullshit. Leonardo da Vinci you can see. Michelangelo you can see. He was an incredible artist to paint that shit and make it look so real. But some of these abstract artists are bullshit.

The same thing happens with poetry. You have anybody thinking that they can write poetry like Maya Angelou and it comes out like garbage. Then you have people confusing poetry with pornography. Here, I'll give you an example:

MY DICK IS MY MAN

a poem by Ed Lover

My dick is my man,
He goes with me wherever I take him.
I let him out for light when I choose to,
But sometimes he makes me do things that I would not otherwise do.

My dick is my man!

He relieves me when I'm tight and full of water.

He brings me into ecstasy with his movements and his thrusts, he is a must.

With nuts I bust,

Sista, do you hear what I'm saying to ya?

That's bullshit!!! I would like to read you another one that caught me last night when I was on the toilet. It's called "My Ass."

MY ASS

My ass is my friend.

It's my rear end.

It's not an entrance,

It's an exit.

It's close to my dick, who's also my man,

But my ass is my friend.

When I'm stuffed up and can't shit,

I give Ex-Lax to it.

My ass is my friend.

Then they'll end the reading with, "You know what I'm sayin'?!" No, I don't know what you're fuckin' sayin'!

Bullshit. I'll tell you in a minute, I ain't dig your shit. That's one thing about me, I'll tell you straight up I didn't dig that or that shit was bullshit. But then I'll tell you I'm not a prayer book. They don't want to hear an honest opinion.

DUN NA NA NA NA NA NA NA— FAT MAN!!!

FIRST and foremost, my weight ain't got nothin' to do with Ed. It's got nothin' to do with my job. It ain't got nothin' to do with nobody else. It has got everything to do with me. It's internal. My problems with weight are mental more than physical. I sat down with six different shrinks. I can explain it, but I can't change it until I'm mentally ready.

If you ever notice, the fat man is always playin' the buffoon. John Candy tried to revolutionize that and change that a little bit. People don't know the real reason he died. He died trying to lose the weight. Everybody was dying for him to lose weight. He died because he lost weight too fast. No, he dropped fifty-three pounds too fast.

That was explained to me. You can't lose it too fast; it's an unnatural state physically, mentally, biologically, and especially emotionally. If you do, your fuckin' heart will overload and kill you. Oprah Winfrey found that out. You can't do it, because your body will go into shock. Mentally you can't do it, because once you feel that you've reached this ideal weight and this ideal look, you might not be the same person you were before. There's plenty of hurt and pain that I've been going through, but it's subsiding as I get older. And I'm beginning to handle a certain situation. I had a strong, deep relationship with my father. That was deeper than I even thought I knew. I felt cheated out of lot of things in life because of his death. And until I settle that in my mind, which I'm doing slowly but surely—and those things are starting to subside—I can learn to accept death for what it is and I can accept anybody's death. I've been around death. I've seen people killed. I've seen people's car accidents. Death doesn't bother me; but the magnitude of the death of my father and the tremendous loss of that male role model changed me. That's the key. And that's the reason it's always hung tight with me. It's not about Ed getting on my nerves a thousand and one times. Yeah, Ed fuckin' frustrates me. *Boom*—and I run to McDonald's. I can't blame him for making me run to McDonald's, my feet brought me into McDonald's; he didn't drive the fuckin' car. He didn't step up over the drive-thru.

It's like trying to say to a drug addict, "Stop doing drugs, stop doing drugs! I'm taking it away from you cold turkey." It's a learned fact: It doesn't work. A lot of my weight is not food, a lot of it is emotion, a lot of it is defense. That's what it is, and when my father passed away I had to assume his role. When my father died, I was just graduating high school. Just graduating high school. My sister had already left for college; she was at Barnett College in Iowa. My brother was going to school and I had a foster brother,

Phillip, who went to Hofstra. I had to give up going on a full scholarship to USC or Syracuse because somebody had to stay home because my mother was in a shambles. My mother was a wreck. The man she lived with for twenty-eight years passed away. My mother never paid a bill in her life, not basic shit, the kinda stuff that came in her name, but she didn't run the household. Usually it was the other way around, where the father came in, throw the check down, the mother take care of the whole thing. My father, you got to understand, my father ran everything. My father tried to stay alive for three more days, and since he died one day ahead of time, they took the fuckin' money off the table!! If he died on the eighth, I would have been granted money to go to school. They would have given me a full ride. Instead he died on the seventh.

That's when the weight became out of control. And you know what, as sudden as it came it will leave. So when people see me, they need to know I'm not this way because I'm lazy or because I eat too much. I'm this way because I've had different life experiences than a lot of other people. I know that's not an excuse, but it's my explanation and as soon as I resolve my feelings surrounding my father's death, I will be able to resolve my weight. Just know that when you talk about me or tease me that I have real feelings also, just like millions of other overweight people.

ED'S FOOD CORNER

I love me some soul food. Big Vi (Mom) gets down for her crown. Everybody thinks their mom is the best cook in the world except for white folks. They pretty much know their moms can't get down at all. Unfortunately, I can't always get mom's home cooking so I order take-out.

I don't care what take-out restaurant you go to, they only give you about three napkins. You can go to a Chinese restaurant and order $500 worth of food and they hit you off with just three napkins. How much can a bag of friggin' napkins cost, that I can only have three of them? They're thin-ass paper napkins too; it's not even Bounty. They look at you like you're crazy if you take more than they give you. With sticky-ass honey chicken that sticks to every finger of each hand, it makes you feel like a freaking webbed octopus man, and they still only give you three napkins. Cheap bastards! They act like they're conserving something. You have to beg them for an extra duck sauce.

And what is duck sauce? I've never seen a duck make sauce. Whatever it is, Black people love it. I don't understand how Chinese people can get a restaurant in a Black neighborhood. Their whole family be working in there. You never understand what you said when they say it. It's like, "Can I have an order of chicken and French fries?" and they say, "Hiawong chung seng che chang fu you." I'm like, Is that what I said? So from now on when I go into a Chinese restaurant I'm gonna ask for just what I heard them say last time: "Fong doe chen fu you."

I'll try anything once when it comes to food. I had alligator, octopus, and I've even had snails before; they call it escargot. Octopus is nasty—it tastes like rubber.

Don't take your girl out to eat nothing like that because she'll just tell you where to go. For instance, women can't eat clams. They're funny like that. God knew what he was doing when he made women because he made them so complex. That's why they're the greatest gift God has given to mankind. The best things are usually complex.

Like, most women don't like beer. My favorite beer is Olde English. I hate Heineken. Heineken is baseball beer. I don't drink that. That's green beer; it comes in a green bottle. Give me some charcoal-filtered ghetto beer. I'd drink more O-E if they served it at clubs. I'm a beer connoisseur. You've got to pour some out for some of the folks who died and are locked down—that's a Black thang.

YOU know we couldn't write a book without telling the whole story

about MTV. See, you were all ready to finish, but here's the real truth

about MTV and what we do at Hot 97.

"ARE YOU DOWN WITH MTV?" "SOMETIMES, GEE!"

—Ed Lover and Todd 1

YO FAMILY

This part should really be called Our Family. Our *Yo! MTV Raps* family. 'Cause this is where we get out the *Yo!* family album—those dusty ol' video reels—and give props to those people who, behind the scenes or in front of the camera, gave *Yo!* its special flavor.

Okay. Get out your hankies. This is the nostalgia part, like when your Moms gets misty looking at your bronze baby shoes.

Dre, your Moms didn't get misty, she pulled a muscle gettin' your bronze baby barges out the closet.

BRAINCHILDREN

Of course, you already heard us mention our man and *Yo!* producer, Ted Demme, whose brainchild concept for a hot, edgy show featuring real hip-hop music—the largest, most hardcore sound of the '80s and '90s—became the first *Yo! MTV Raps* show. You already know that Ted saw in us what we didn't even know we were: the hip-hop ambassadors to the world! And you know that we didn't even know each other. But this is about Ted. So, you tell 'em, Ed!

Okay, Dre. The real deal: Me and Ted were buddies in high school. And I sure as hell didn't know that, someday, that nerdy kid Ted was gonna be a hot producer at MTV and that my career as class clown was gonna take off because of him. So, from the bottom of my heart, thanks, Ted! And I'm sorry about the stink bomb in your locker.

We also gotta give a shout out to Peter Dougherty. He launched *Yo!* with Ted. Before he moved on, he was always there for us. He was real, he had our backs. He was old school *Yo!,* where it all began.

YO! MAILMAN

THE T-MONEY TREE

Ed, did you ever notice how many of our guests and regulars on *Yo!* seemed to look like our old friend and *Yo!* sidekick, T-Money? Sometimes it was enough to make me wonder . . .

Exactly right, Dre. A strange coincidence. Hold on! Let's count 'em up!

First and foremost, Ed, there was Yo! Mailman. Neither rain, nor sleet, nor any amount of bull, could keep that courier from makin' his rounds.

Some of what he brought was kinda wack. Some weird-ass stuff. But no doubt about it, Yo! Mailman delivered the mail, rain or shit!

Remember poor ol' Uncle BoBo Lovetree? More like one of T-Money's relatives. After he won that $700 million lottery he got really large—called himself "Sweet Daddy" Uncle BoBo Lovetree. Fancy women, fancy cars, fancy-ass.

PooR Uncle BoBo LoveTRee

Didn't see much of him after that. Well, that's show biz, Ed. Good thing you missed that last-minute guest and T-Money look-alike, Fred Lincoln. He was plugging *Fred Lincoln's Book of Infinite Knowledge*. Good timing, getting the flu, Ed.

Then there was that janitor guy, Clarence Coldwater Capsule. Kept the

Fred Lincoln

Yo! set clean. He was kinda expensive. Hadda let him go when they cut our budget. And remember that Jamaican brother, Donovan Money?

Blunted most of the time, Ed.

What about Derek—World's Greatest Athlete? That brother competed in every single Olympic event. Don't think he won nothin', though.

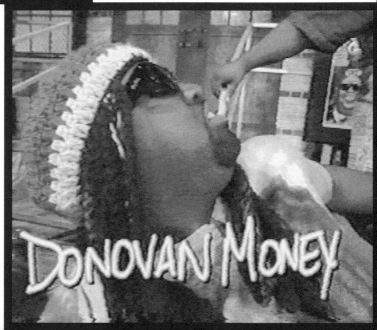

And don't forget *Yo!*'s own superhero, the Nubianator. That dude had juice, stamping out crime in the 'hood!

D.J. Slik had juice, too.

Not that kinda juice, Dre! Always spraying that hair-grease shit all over everything.

Coulda used ol' Clarence Coldwater Capsule to clean up some of Slik's mess. And who could forget Aunt Francine? She was something else, pregnant at her age.

Damn, Dre! You had to bring that up? Took my ass to family court . . .

The Nubianator

And whenever the Christmas season rolls around, Ed, I always think of our visit from Santana Clause.

Yeah, Dre, he really put me in a holiday mood. Feliz Navidad, bro!

T-Money, as Santana Clause, delivers holiday cheer from the South Pole of Mexico in a "Cheby" to <u>Yo!</u>

Santana Clause

THE SHOW THAT LAUNCHED A THOUSAND YO'S!

Y'all know *Yo!* wasn't just any video show! We gave people information and the history behind the music. We gave viewers catalogues on some of the albums, so they would know where these records came from and where they went. We also made shit funny—did skits just for our audience, with guest stars and heroes for our generation. We made people laugh and say, "Damn! Those niggas are funny!"

The thing was, we went in there and revolutionized the channel. Actually, Ted Demme revolutionized the channel. When we got in, we joined Ted and Peter Dougherty and helped build their vision, which became our vision also. They allowed us to come in and give our thoughts and help mold the way MTV is looked at today.

This is an example of us molding our vision of <u>Yo! MTV Raps.</u> Actually, it's an example of Ice-T, molding us. That's yours truly, hangin' wit' Ice T—upside down. Bad-ass barges onto our set, poppin' shit, and ties us up. Ed's still got the marks on his face. Holding us for ransom 'til we played his damn video . . .

We always busted our ass trying to please our viewers 'cause that's what kept us going. Unfortunately, we also had to please our producers and management. With all that pleasing comes conflict. And exhaustion. And some damn weird outfits. In this picture, believe it or not, me and Dre and T-Money're trying to create a wholesome, sophisticated late-night family show for idealistic gangsta revolutionary teenagers who are into rap and yoga.

Ed, you left out the part about "in support of vegetarian school-lunch programs." Let me tell y'all, there were days when I felt like a human wishbone tryin' to do the right thing.

I can assure you, you never looked like no wishbone, Doctor. But you're right, we put up a good fight . . . playing hip-hop ya hadda respect.

Don't forget, Ed, when it came to production, MTV always gave us carte blanche. Anything we wanted for our show, first they'd blanch, then we had to cart it our own damn selves! We were welcome to any of the props and shit from the other shows—whatever they weren't using. Nevertheless, *Yo! MTV Raps,* running prime-time five days a week, was on top for years; we were the most-watched show on that channel, and we pulled in the big advertising dollars.

A perfect example of recycling on the <u>Yo!</u> set: We were forced to borrow these outfits from Kurt Loder when MTV cut our wardrobe budget. The hat Dre stole from Cindy Crawford. We raided the president's office for the mugs— the tea bags came from somebody's take-out. Tough shit! This is about art, man!

And you can't hardly tell, Dre, that our budget was just this side of a Little Rascals barn show. It's whatcha call style—down-with-Dre-and-Ed style. Right?

Think we're kidding? How many TV shows do you know where they give you Monopoly money for your production budget? That's right! Damn Monopoly money!

THE FAME GAME

S'right. So ends were short on the set. That didn't stop me and Dre from turnin' into household words. Fact is, Dre turned into a whole household all by himself. As newborn celebs from *Yo! MTV Raps,* we had the opportunity to meet and greet and be interviewed by the best! Here are just a few examples of how we played the fame game.

Formerly Down with Ed

I don't exactly remember where I met the artist formerly known as Prince (from now on I'll call him P for short since I don't have that symbol on my typewriter), but we got to be cool when I was in L.A. Me and Dre were in an L.A. club and we saw Eddie Murphy, Arsenio Hall, and P. Dre said, "Go over there and talk to Prince." I was like, "Nah, man. He ain't gonna talk to me." Dre went on, "What's the worst thing he can say to you? Nothing." So I went over to where P was and by the time I got there he was on the dance floor. So I went out on the dance floor and introduced myself and we started talkin'. We had a cool conversation. I met his bodyguard Big Chick and everything. The next day I found out we were staying in the same hotel and by coincidence my phone rang. "Yo! Who's this?" P was like, "It's Prince." I was like, "Yo! What's up P! I saw Chick downstairs." P was like, "I know, man. What you doin' tonight—we're hangin' out. You want to come?" I was like, "I'm with it!" That night we went to the China Club and hung out. We became real cool. Later on P did a performance for MTV and I was in the front row groovin' and P threw me a symbol and said, What's up. So I told everyone at MTV that me and P was cool. Everybody was like, "Sure, Ed. You're cool with Prince. Yeah right!" No one believed me except Dre. Boy, did I show them! P's band, the New Power Generation, was rehearsing for his performance at the MTV Music Awards and I happened to walk in. I saw P sitting in the middle of an empty row with his bodyguard Big

Chick on one end and another guard on the other end. I say, "What's up" to everyone on the staff and they sarcastically reply, "Ed, there's your man Prince. You know, your good friend. Why don't you go and say hi!" I shrugged my shoulders and said, "Okay." I walked down the aisle to where P was sitting and gave Big Chick a pound and said, "What's up." P saw me and waved his hand and Big Chick moved and let me into the row. I sat down next to P and I can hear everybody behind me goin', "Oh shit! He really knows Prince." By this time the band finished performing and Prince turned to me and asked me, "Ed, what did you think about that song?" I go, "They were alright, but the drummer was a little off. I think they can be a little tighter." P stood up and said, "Ed said y'all was fucked up!" The whole MTV crew was like, "Oh shit!" You remember that show—it was the one where P wore that bad-ass suit with his bad ass hangin' out. That's my man!

Anybody sayin' I ain't down with the Artist Formerly Known as (know what I'm sayin'?) don't know shit!

You got that right, Ed. And if you don't believe him, you can ask James Brown!

The Godfather Speaks...

WE were doing *Yo! MTV Raps* and we were all excited and hyped up because James Brown was coming on our show. James Brown came and we did a week's worth of shows with him. We were on the set and I had to teach him to do the Ed Lover Dance and I'm hyped because this is the Godfather of Soul and I'm showing him how to do the Ed Lover Dance. Then he starts showing me how to do his dance and Dre plays all his music and he's doing his thing. All these photographers are there and we're thanking him for coming and telling him how much of a pleasure it was to have him on the show. How there would be no rap music if it wasn't for him because there would be no beats and so on. After we taped the last show I was in my dressing room and James had left the studio. Dre comes in and asks me, "Did you understand any goddamn thing he said to us the whole damn week??!!" I sat there for a minute and I realized I didn't understand a damn thing James had said to us. For the whole time he was there you could see we didn't understand a damn thing he said. We just had these blank looks on our faces and we nodded a lot. He was like, "Tha's musac na na dun bum rap musac and it's good. Na ha nag had ba da la ta good!"

The Godfather. He's still one of my biggest heroes. Hanging with the Godfather has made me wonder if maybe things're better when you don't understand everything a person says. There was one time on *Yo!* I know Ed and I wished this was true. It had to do with Larry Fishburne.

Noise in the 'Hood

WE had just moved from our first *Yo!* set to our second one. We were talking about *Boyz N the Hood* because it had just come out, and we were making random jokes about the cast. We especially made comments about Larry Fishburne. "Larry Fishburne wasn't nothin'. He wasn't even good in *Cornbread, Earl and Me*—he couldn't even play me." Everybody on the set kept feeding us things to say about Larry Fishburne. All of a sudden a guy in a cape, a mask, and a cane comes running out from backstage screaming and yelling. Dre and I are in shock and we were sitting there looking like two scared little boys. Everyone was cracking up because they set us up! Larry Fishburne was backstage the whole time waiting for his cue.

Face it, Ed. That was a setup—pure and simple. Since then, I, at least, learned to look both ways before mouthing off.

What d'ya mean, "I, at least"?

'Cause I still only know of one occasion that ever left my man Ed Lover speechless.

Shaq Attack

SHAQ was a rookie when he came on *Yo!* so Dre and I came up with this idea of how to work Shaq into the show. I came out wearing these wild clothes and saying that I just got cut by the Orlando Magic. Dre was like, "Well, why did you get cut, man?" "I done tried out for every team in the NBA and the only ones that were going to put me on was the Orlando Magic so I'm on the team and they cut me for some big, stupid scrub named O'Neal, O'Neal somebody. Shaquille Big Dummy O'Neal, you can't outball me." And Shaq walks in, and Dre is like, "Ed, this is Shaquille O'Neal." And I'm like, "Oh, hi, Shaq, I wasn't talkin' too much stuff about you, was I?"

I still can't believe he did that shit! Scrubbin' me with a kiss...

And from nowhere he just leans over and kisses me right on the face. And I just fell right on the floor.

Damn, Dre! Bad enough that shit was broadcast worldwide. Now you have to remind everybody all over again in our book? So happens, I remember that a certain Doctor I know would do anything for fame. C'mon, Drizzay. 'Fess up.

Dre's #1 Bellyflop

DURING one of the first Spring Breaks Julie Brown hosted a top-ten video show. Ed told Julie that I had a crush on her and that I would do anything for her. Ed told Julie, "You know what? Dre will paint a #1 on his belly and jump in the pool announcing the #1 video just for you. That's how much he likes you." I'm shaking my head and saying, "No I won't." After an hour of coaxing, Ed and Ted convinced me to do it. So I paint the #1 on my stomach and Ted and Ed are on the side saying, "If you do this, you don't understand, we'll be so famous. You'll blow up. You'll be the highlight of MTV!" Meanwhile I'm standing there with a big #1 on my belly saying, "I don't know about this, you guys." They're cracking up, going, "No, no. Trust us, you'll be famous." Next thing you know, they're announcing the #1 video. I walk up this long runway and Julie announces, "Now it's time for the #1 video, and as we announce the video, Doctor Dre is going to jump in the pool." Everyone is going wild now because they see me at the end of the runway

with this big-ass #1 painted on my belly. So I think to myself, "I might as well milk this for everything it's got." So I walk around the pool and let everyone see me. The crowd is screaming, "Jump! Jump! Jump!" I go back to the runway and finally the big moment arrives and I run and jump. I hit the water and SPLASH!!!! Everyone is laughing and Ted and Ed are on the floor in tears. Once again Dre has been had.

Okay, Ed. Even! But sometimes we didn't go after fame. Sometimes it came after us. Like the time the Chairman tracked you down.

Quaking in My Boots

TED called me at home one day and said, "Somebody from Bill Cosby's office called for you and here's the number." So I call the number, all the while thinking, "Why the hell would Bill Cosby be calling me?" The one thing that stood out in my mind was something I remembered from Eddie Murphy's stand-up routine: "Bill Cosby only calls you for one of two reasons. Either he really likes you a lot and he wants to tell you he likes you, or he really hates you a lot and he wants to tell you how much he hates you." The bad thing about it was that this happened right after an article came out in *Word Up!* magazine calling Dre and me buffoons and we were really upset about that and then Bill Cosby calls. So I'm thinking, "This man is about to rip me to shreds. I admire him and he's about to kill me." So I call his office and his assistant Kim answers the phone. I go, "Hi! My name is Ed Lover and somebody called me from your office." She goes, "Oh, yeah! Hi, Ed! This is Kim. I'm Mr. Cosby's assistant. Hold on, Bill wants to speak to you." She puts me on hold and I'm sitting in my little Jersey City apartment going, "Hell no! Bill Cosby isn't going to get on this telephone. Somebody else is going to get on the phone, tell me what he wanted to tell me, and that will be it." The phone clicks back over and I hear, "HELLO, ED!" I go, "Mr. Cosby?" "No, Bill. Please call me Bill. Yes, this is Bill Cosby." I go, "I can't believe it! I can't believe it!" "What's wrong wit' ya, Ed?!" I said, "I'm kinda nervous. It's weird talking to someone you've idolized for so long." I start shaking all over. He

My man Bill made good on his word. Here I am on his show.

goes, "What, are you shivering? You sound like you're shivering. Well, just turn on the damn heat in your room, then. Okay. Well, listen, I got the kids, and you know I got my wife, Camille. And my wife, Camille, and we got three lovely kids, and I love my kids dearly. Now, I got a daughter and she just goes on and on, 'Daddy, *Yo! MTV Raps* this' and '*Yo! MTV Raps* that' and 'Daddy, you've just got to see *Yo! MTV Raps*.' So I'm sitting in my office one day and I don't have anything to do so I'm turning the channels on my TV and there's you and the big fat jolly guy there and he's running around and you're doing your thing. You've got on this character thing that you were doing and you have this huntin'-lookin' hat on and the glasses with the tape in the middle." I say, "Yeah, that's Perry J. Perrywinkle. That's one of the characters I do." He goes, "Oh! I'm on the floor, man, just on the floor, and this guy, your partner—what's his name, Doctor Grey?" I'm like, "No, Doctor Dre." Bill's like, "Okay, Doctor Dre. Well, anyway, he don't know what you're talking about and you're spitting all over him. Man, I laughed so hard. I was just laughing. Man, you guys are just terrific!" I say, "Well, thank you, Mr. Cosby." And he goes, "Now. This is what we're gonna do. I'm gonna come on your show and then I'm gonna have you on my show. All right?! Now you set that up." I'm going, "Okay, Mr. Cosby. Hold on for a minute." I have three-way calling so I call Ted. I go, "Ted, you're not going to believe this, but I have Bill Cosby on the other line right now." He's like, "You're a fuckin' liar." I say, "No, Ted, Bill Cosby's on the other line and he wants to be on *Yo!*" Ted's going, "Umm, ummm, tell him Thursday." I click over and say, "Mr. Cosby . . ." He goes, "No, no, no, I told you to call me Bill. Bill." I go, "Okay, Bill, can you come down Thursday?" He goes, "What time?" I'm like, "Oh, shit! Hold on, Bill." I click over and say, "Ted, what time?!" Ted goes, "Oh shit." He starts shuffling through some papers and says, "One o'clock." I click over and say, "Bill, how's Thursday at one o'clock?" He goes, "No, Thursday at one o'clock isn't good. We're shooting at one o'clock on Thursday. How about Wednesday?" All the while I knew we didn't tape *Yo!* on Wednesday, but I said, "Okay." So everybody is on the *Yo!* set that Wednesday, and I mean everybody. Assistants I've never seen are on hand for this shoot. The press is there, food, and the whole nine. It was about 1:15 and Bill hadn't arrived yet so everybody was ragging on me. "Ed, you're a liar. Bill Cosby ain't coming." I walk off the set and decide to take a walk. As I go outside, a cab pulls up and out comes Bill Cosby all by himself! I couldn't believe it—no entourage. He walks up to me and shakes my hand for a couple of minutes and says, "Hi, Ed. Nice to meet you." All I could do was stare and shake my head up and down. We go into the studio and of course everybody surrounds Bill and sort of pushes me off to the side. Bill says, "Let's get started." So we start doing our thing, but there are so many people around that we have to retake the shoot a couple of times. Bill pulls me to the side and says, "Are there always this many people on the set while you're taping the show?" I go, "No. I don't know half of these people and the rest never show up while we're shooting." Bill then says, "Everybody off the set except for the cameraman and the producer." Everybody left and we went on to tape several segments with no re-takes. I can definitely say that was one of the coolest things ever to happen to us.

Ed, you know what happens to folks like us always hangin' with famous people?

Yeah. Robin Leach happens to us. Sooner or later, you're bound to get Leached!

You know you in the house when my man Robin Leach pays you a visit. We were making all the moves, lifestyling like royalty. It's not on a par with winning the lottery, but it's definitely a sign you got it goin' on in high places. Right, Dre?

In this picture, Ed has joined me and my guest, Robin, in my study for a spot of tea . . . Okay, scratch the tea part. We had just sent out for KFC, and Ed's having an Old E. I think Robin was spiking his RC Cola from one of those Brit hip flasks.

YO! GETS AROUND

WHEN you're the hosts of *Yo! MTV Raps,* doors really open for you. Of course, sometimes they got slammed just as soon as someone sees our asses standing on their stoop. "Oh, shit! It's those bad-ass, gangsta, celebrity rap dudes!" But none of that's ever stood in our way. We in the house, one way or the other! But you gotta have a plan. You gotta have a plan.

Like how we got on Arsenio's show . . .

My Bodyguard Can Beat Up Your Bodyguard

REMEMBER when you knew you were the shit when you made it on *The Arsenio Hall Show?* Well, the way we got on *The Arsenio Hall Show* was a little different than most people. First we had our manager, Charlie, call the Arsenio Hall people and try to get us on the show. They told him, "We're not interviewing those kind of people right now." We were like, "What the fuck does 'those kind of people' mean?!" We were heated. We spotted Arsenio at the MTV Music Awards soon after that and decided it

was time to have a little talk. Arsenio had a bodyguard on one side of him and his personal assistant on the other. We decided to stage a distraction, so we had Dre's brother Fred try to push into the row on the side where Arsenio's bodyguard was sitting. When his bodyguard got up to check things out we climbed down from two rows behind him and sat right next to Arsenio. *BOOM!* We were like, "Arsenio, when are you going to let us be on your show?" The next night we told the world how we got on *The Arsenio Hall Show* from guess where? Arsenio's couch. You couldn't tell us nothing'!

That was some funny shit. Just shows where there's a will, there's a way. 'Course, Dre knows there's times the shit you say can fly right back in your face . . .

Boomerang

WE'RE doin' a contest for MTV for *Boomerang* with Eddie Murphy, and we're sittin' out in the Paramount lot and we're talkin' to Eddie. Picture this: It's the middle of the day in Los Angeles and it's like 110 degrees out there. So, we're talkin' to Eddie Murphy and I'm like, "Tell me about *Boomerang,*" and he's going, "It's a wonderful film with wonderful people and it's just going to be wonderful. So go down to the wonderful movie house and take that wonderful money outta your pocket and just spend it on this wonderfulness. And this film is just gonna be wonderful." And I'm laughing about it. And Dre goes,

"Well, you know it's hot and I know you got to be hot out here." Eddie turns to Dre and says, "Well, I'm not the one standing out here in a leather shirt." Dre had a *Yo! MTV Raps* leather shirt on zipped all the way the fuck up to his collar. With sweat pouring off his head.

Hey, it was a matter of style. And I needed a little profiling, after my "guest star" role on *The Fresh Prince.* What I'm saying, don't believe the hype about all this Hollywood glamour.

Bull in Bel Air

BASICALLY, Will Smith gave me a call and said, "We're doing a show with a bunch of different doctors. I have a dream in the show where I'm being treated by all these different doctors who happen to be soap opera and stage doctors and I want you to play Doctor Dre and do a rap." So I say, "Sure, why not." When I get there I read the script and it said: "Doctor Dre: Dre will supply the rap." Well, I sat there and said, "Damn, you got the wrong

guy." The first thing I did was call Ed. "Yo! Ed, ED, they want me to do some kinda freestyle rhyme." Ed said, "Okay. What's it about?" Of course all I could say was, "I don't know. I'll call you back as soon as I find out." Most of the week we went through rehearsals and my part kept getting put off. Will kept going, "Dre, don't worry, we'll work it out." So I'm thinking, Okay, more time for me to try to get next to Karyn Parsons. That didn't work so I started to compare stomach size and clothing with Uncle Phil, James Avery. That got boring so Alfonso Rivera and I started to out–Michael Jackson each other to death. You know, the steps, the scream, the whole bit. All the while Will was running in and out trying to get everything together. "Don't worry, Dre, your part is going to be phat. Jazzy is working on the music and everything is going to be phat." I was thinking that if worse came to worst I would just call Ed. Wednesday rolled around and once again we were up to my part. They started playing the music and Will turned to me and said, "Okay Dre, throw a phat freestyle rhyme on us!" I turned around and said, "Let me hear the music some more and catch the vibe." In my mind I was thinking, How long can I stall until I can get to a phone to call Ed? Everybody started looking at me and Will said, "Don't worry, we'll write this for you." Thursday rolled around and I pulled Will aside and said, "Do we have the rhyme yet?" He went, "Don't worry, we're working on it. You can do a walk-through today and it'll be fine tomorrow." That night Will gave me a rhyme at the last minute and said, "Here. Do this." Anyone who knows me knows I'm not the rapper, Ed is, and you just can't give someone a rhyme and expect it to come off. So I read it: "I'm Doctor Dre, got the vicious swirl. Will I'm gonna make you go to hell??!" Everyone looked at me like, That's it, that's the best you could come up with? Will breaks the silence. "I think we'll rewrite this." Of course I ran to the phone and called Ed and Charlie. Sweating bullets, I told them the whole story and how I thought they were going to write me out. Finally, after a change in music, a new rap, and five takes, we got it.

Whoa! Wait a minute, Dre. I went to the Super Bowl that year and seemed to remember seeing Will Smith there. He just happened to mention to me how he damn near fell asleep in the hospital bed because you couldn't remember your lines!

One time Ed and me were invited to be guests of honor at the Playboy Club in Vegas. It was a struggle—what with our busy schedule—but in the end, we felt we couldn't disappoint all those honeys, so we made the scene. Know what I'm sayin'? Whatever . . .

Yeah, right, Dre. Good thing we did go, 'cause that night the Doctor made scientific history. You know how folks talk about the night they saw Halley's Comet and shit? This was like that. Definitely a night to remember.

A Star Lands

WE were in a water park in Vegas and Dre and I went on this water slide that was about ten stories high. The slide goes straight down until you get to the bottom and then it empties out into this pool. We walk up the slide with our friend Glenn. We get all the way to the top of the slide and I figure I'll be Captain Braveheart and go down first. I'm flyin' down the slide at about seventy-five miles an hour and come out the bottom. *Vooom!* I'm so light I skid across the water and finally go under about ten inches from the edge of the pool. I'm laughin'. Then Glenn comes down. Glenn is about 6'7" and weighs about 235–240 pounds. Glenn comes flyin' down the slide and shoots out and plunges in the water. *Ba-boom!* Water flies all over the place. Then

That's me with my man Giggy standing next to the world's largest living projectile, the one and only Doctor Dre. Look at the man! He's grinning like he got the key to a Brink's truck: He just caused the biggest wet T-shirt contest in the history of the Playboy Club.

we both turn around and where's Dre? Still at the top of the slide. We're yelling to Dre, "Go! Go! Do it! Do it!" He looks over the edge and backs up and shakes his head no. By now two or three people go in front of him. We're yelling to him, "Do it! Do it! Jump!" By this time the whole park stopped what they were doing and were at the bottom of this slide yelling to Dre, "Jump! Jump! Jump!" Finally, Dre gets on the slide and Dre's weight creates the velocity of a wind tunnel. He must have been coming down this slide at about 160 miles per hour. He shot out of the slide and didn't even touch the water and got about two feet away from where the pool ended, hit the water and **BOOOOM!!!** Like a tidal wave the water rose from the pool and everybody in that park got drenched. It seemed like it was raining for several minutes.

Halley's Comet. Thanks, Ed. Why don't you tell everybody about the science history you witnessed with RuPaul.

More like *Ripley's Believe It or Not*, Doctor.

Anatomy Lesson

ONE time we were at Spring Break and RuPaul had a tent and he wouldn't let anybody else but him and his makeup person go in the tent when he was getting ready to get RuPauled. It takes like hours for him to transform into RuPaul because he has to shave all the hair off his face and legs. They really go at this thing a long time. So I remember walkin' down there asking everybody, "What's in the tent?" And they're tellin' me, "Ed, don't go in the tent!" Of course I don't listen. I open the thing, go in the tent, and there's RuPaul, and his makeup person is grabbing his thing—what I saw was RuPaul standing there with his legs wide open while the other guy was on his knees with his hands underneath like pulling his shit so they could tie it down. I was like, "Oh, God, I'm so sorry." I couldn't even watch. I just turned around real quick and walked out.

THE ED LOVER DANCE!!!

THE Ed Lover Dance was created in or about 1990. The dance was the brainchild of the man who was the third leg of *Yo! MTV Raps,* the genius known to you all as T-Money. T showed me the dance one day between takes during the filming of the show. I checked it out, added a few bumps of my own, and created something that would soon take the country by storm. Dre was the one who suggested I use the music of "The 900 Number" by DJ Mark the 45 King. Soon everywhere I went people would ask me to do the Ed Lover Dance. Sometimes it was cool; other times it got on my damn nerves, making me wish I'd never done the dance in the first place. But check this out: I devised a way to keep myself from always having to do the dance. I made the announcement that the Ed Lover Dance would and could only be performed on Wednesday. Why? The hell if I know!! So when people would ask me to do the dance, if I didn't feel like it and it wasn't Wednesday I had an excuse! To this day, whenever I'm in a club and the DJ puts on "The 900 Number," everybody will turn to me to see if I'm going to do the Ed Lover Dance.

Did You Know?

- Ed once did the Ed Lover Dance underwater!
- The largest number of people ever to do the Ed Lover Dance at one time exceeds seventeen thousand!
- Bobby Brown, M.C. Hammer, and the Godfather of Soul, James Brown, as well as comedian Bill Cosby have all received lessons in the Ed Lover Dance from the master, Ed Lover himself!!!

The Ed Lover Dance's got juice with Arsenio

TO RUSSIA WITH <u>YO!</u> (AND CHICKEN KIEV)

ME and Dre were invited to perform at a music festival in St. Petersburg, Russia. We came with the *Yo!* crew, so the New World Order could be down wit' *Yo! MTV Raps*. Salt-n-Pepa came, too. It is called the White Nights Festival. This is a great honor. First, we had to go to a little pre-party at the Russian Tea Room in New York to discuss this honor. And practice drinking vodka.

When I found out Ed and I were going to Russia, I'll admit it: I was a little nervous. You know, you hear shit—cold wars, spies, superpowers, nuclear stuff. But when I landed at the St. Petersburg airport, I found out it was all hype. All these hooptie old airplanes lying around the airfield. The main terminal was so old, it made buildings in the South Bronx look like some kinda country club. The conveyor belt was made of wood. It made noises like a moose with a hernia. Customs officials filled out

This is us at the old Tea Room getting a few pointers in diplomacy from our man Henry Kissinger. First thing he told us, "Stay away from the red caviar. It's nasty!" He also told us to bring our own toilet paper.

visas with a damn nib pen. Getting our posse through customs took longer than launching the Space Shuttle. One thing, for sure: The Russians got some superpower hype goin' on!

Truth is, when I heard about this festival, Drizzay, I thought they were saying "white knights." I pictured some kinda guys wearing bedsheets, and I said, "Hell, no!" But the real idea behind the "white nights" is to party all night. That's 'cause St. Petersburg is so far north that, smack in the middle of the summer, the sun just about never sets. Something to do with northern lights and being near the Arctic Circle. That's what they mean by white nights. For real, it's more like light-gray nights. Let me tell you, that shit'll really fuck you up. No one knows if they're goin' to work or comin' home. And after a face full of vodka, they don't give a damn, neither!

Just before our White Knights performance, I strolled around the festival grounds to check out the fans. A mob! At least ten thousand kids made the scene! Half of them were

I'm inspecting the hi-tech accommodations at the St. Petersburg airport. Maintenance is done by little old ladies called <u>babushkas</u>. They got a rag tied around their mop and another one 'round their head. This was thought up by a Russian efficiency expert. This way, they can clean the ceiling the same time they mop the floor.

Midnight in St. Petersburg, and it looks like high noon. No shit!! That's what time it really is behind my ass!

See what I mean? This is me, Salt, Pepa, and Spinderella at some fancy-ass festival reception. We're full of vodka and lookin' tired and mean. Stuff like this has been going on for days. I am serious about this—they ain't got no nights! But there's always some guy passing chicken Kiev hors d'oeuvres.

waiting across the road by the Russian Military Museum. Full of rusty old tanks and cannons. Kids from St. Petersburg like to throw rave parties in there. Another reason to party all night. Dre and me went the night before. That was some wild shit, but we left early. Right after the local chapter of the mafia showed up for their surcharge on the fun.

Let me tell you, the Russians will grab any excuse to party. And they go at it like they're under siege. These folks are very intense when it comes to having a good time. It helps keep their minds off things like they ain't got nothin' to eat but chicken Kiev. Come to think about it, they're very intense about everything. Maybe it's the vodka . . .

One thing that blew my mind during the show: the Russian kids may not know what mothafucka means, but money, they know the words to every rap!

The Doctor's traffic jam, Russian style. Piece of cake, once they got my wheels of steel up and running. In Russia, it's the same as lampin': Two vacuum cleaner cords run into a battery in the men's room 'cross the way and <u>zow!</u> We got juice!

But not enough juice for a real green room, Dre. Those Russian promoters gave us army tents. None of the American honeys on our tour were thrilled about getting ready in something too cramped for a Boy Scout. I'm telling the Pentagon, you wanna roll on the Russian Army, just wait 'til they're in their tents. Can't even stand up in those little suckers.

One thing about Russia blew me away, Dre. Truth is, things are very rough. The food sucks. Flying in from Finland, we were eating like kings on the plane. Only half an hour away. In St. Petersburg, folks' groceries are pretty scarce. Except for chicken Kiev. People stand in line for ice cream. Ain't even Häagen-Dazs. They count everything out. You walk into a restaurant—sixteen in your posse. They say, "Sorry, we only got fifteen chicken Kievs." Good thing I left when I did, or I'd have feathers sprouting from my ass.

Livin' large on the czar! Ed and me, and T-Money are resting after a family-size helping of Russian culture. We're sitting in some little nook in the Hermitage. The part you can't see covers an area big as ten shopping malls. Wall-to-wall marble and gold. Kneeling: Salt-n-Pepa's homies, Flipper and Gerald, trying to raise some ends, so they don't have to fly home on Aeroflot.

This is when we called a press conference at the Hotel ——— (too hard to pronounce, impossible to spell) to suggest that Russia better hurry and give up the paint concession to Sherwin Williams. 'Cause when Sherwin Williams says they cover the world, they sure as hell ain't referring to Russia. Describing Russia's like talking about Prince. You gotta say shit like, "We're in a building formerly known as blue." Maybe we need to study this diplomacy stuff a little more . . .

Ed, you gotta say this about Russians: They love art. We went to a lot of art museums in St. Petersburg. They've got stuff you wouldn't believe, and it's all stored in palaces and cathedrals. In the Workers' Paradise, it seems like art lives better than the workers. One place was called the Hermitage. Damn! It used to belong Catherine the Great. Now I see why they call her great. That place was something else!

FROM THE PEOPLE WHO BROUGHT YOU <u>YO!</u>

THE trouble is Ed and me got more ideas than there is time to say them. Crazy stuff just flies out of our mouths like a geyser. Sometimes we catch ahold of it before it disappears and it turns into an episode for *Yo!* or Beauty and the Beach or Spring Break. Sometimes it winds up as a concept for a show or flick, like *Who's the Man?* This next part is a flash peek at some of the other things that also came out of our bag of tricks.

<u>Da Show</u>'s the Thing

ONE time, Dre, Ted, and I sat down and schemed because MTV told us, "Why don't you guys come up with some other stuff—show ideas?"

Okay, we came up with *Da Show*. Real cutting edge. A late-night talk show for MTV. For the first pilot we got Roseanne, not because somebody from talent and artist relations got her, no! Because Ted, Dre, and Ed got on the phone and got

I'm teaching Leslie Nielsen the Ed Lover Dance on <u>Da Show</u>. No doubt about it, we tore it up!

Me and Lover welcome Roseanne and Tom Arnold to <u>Da Show</u>. In this picture, Ed feels a little left out. It just dawned on him that people of SIZE are the true majority. Yo, Ed, have a banana. Get with the program.

Roseanne, John Amos, and Faith No More, and we did the show. And on top of that, Tom Arnold accompanied Roseanne.

The next two "pilot" shows we did at Spring Break. Tony! Toni! Toné! was the house band and the guests included Jean-Claude Van Damme and Leslie Nielsen. We taped these shows, and MTV aired them, and *Da Show* became—like everything else out of our incredibly wild minds—very highly rated. So MTV got some young guy (and you know who!) to host the concept. Of course, they had to rename *Da Show* . . . So, now you know the real deal.

Our Sporting Life

ANOTHER Lover/Doctor brainstorm: Ed, Ted, and I were the ones who started Rock N Jock soft-ball and Rock N Jock basketball, even though we only went to the first one. Yo! Einstein only *wrote* the theory of relativity. When you're a genius, it's so relative, you don't need to stick around. While we were there, Ed played in the basketball game, and we coached with Kareem!

MC Rags

LIKE, before there was clothing like Karl Kani, FUBU, Mecca, or Phat Farm, there was Starter gear. We were getting gear from a guy at Starter to wear on *Yo! MTV Raps*—like the satin sports jackets that Run-D.M.C. wore. Like the Los Angeles Raiders jacket that Chuck D made famous. Ted called up to get us more, but MTV decided that we couldn't show the Starter logo, so we left the tag on the hat. Just us bein' sly. Yo! Does that sound like a look to you? Ever notice how hip-hop kids have this thing about tags? Wonder where they came up wit' that. 'Cause we got letters from kids 24–7 about where did we get our clothes, et cetera.

Naturally, *Yo! MTV* trendsetters like us would have liked to be their spokespeople. But Starter told us they only dealt with sports figures.

So how come later, in the heart of the African-American community, on Jamaica Avenue, in Queens, New York, we look up and see MTV VJ Duff as poster girl for Starter, wearing a Starter shirt? She never wore a Starter shirt in her life. Gee, Ed, I don't think she's on anybody's NFL, NBA, or NHL team, either. Go figure.

WHERE'S THE BEEF?

No '90s-style book would be complete without some insider dirt, some bitchin'. Right? So, here's some beef still sticks in our throats, no matter how hard we try to play it off. The MTV Video Music Awards.

Every year it's said by the big brass, "The jocks aren't going to do anything on the stage. Jocks aren't giving out any of the awards." So how come we're sitting there at Radio City Music Hall and . . . here comes Pauly Shore? That was about three years ago. Pauly's our man, so we're happy for him, but we're wondering what's going on. Another time, Bill Bellamy walks across the stage and he gives out an award. Then Daisy Fuentes. You get the picture. The pioneers of hip-hop programming, the hottest music for two decades, the veterans of *Yo! MTV Raps,* the longest-running show, etc., etc., etc. . . . We're talking about yours truly, Ed and the Doctor, and we never did give out an award! Can you believe that? Especially, never gave out the rap music award. Never! Once! What's up with that?

HOW QUICKLY THEY FORGET

Few of the MTV executives, producers, or staff were on the set for our farewell party. Yo! Was it something we said?

But we still want to take this opportunity to say thank you for all the years, and for the opportunities you helped to create for us, thanks. Something we left MTV without getting. We left out thanking people by name as a sign of respect. But thanks for the good times and the great times. We'll never forget MTV because that's where we got our big start and, unlike some other people, we will always remember where we came from and give thanks where thanks is due.

Thank you, MTV.

"THIS IS SOMETHIN' FOR THE RADIO!"

—Biz Markie,
"Something for the Radio"

ONE day Paco Lopez of Hot 97 called our manager, Charlie, when Hot 97 was changing its programming from a dance format to a hip-hop format. He told Charlie that the station was looking for hosts for the morning show and that we'd be perfect. The next thing we knew, Charlie had heard from Program Director Steve Smith and that was the beginning of the new Hot 97. We were straight up off the cuff and people loved it! Things just got bigger and bigger. We went top three within nine months of when we started in sixteenth place on November 11, 1993.

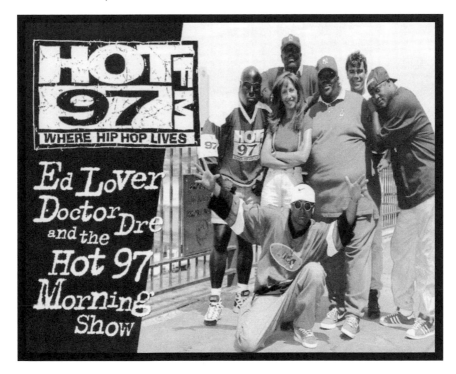

WHEN we first started at Hot 97 we didn't understand the power of our appeal to our audience. We love our *Morning Show* listeners because they're who we are. We represent a minority of people who have long been silenced and now have emerged. You can see that in our ratings. We're the #1 morning music show!

We definitely believe in being creative and constantly come up with new ideas for the show. We know our audience and what they want. A lot of the radio jocks on other stations sound alike. Our audience doesn't want that. They want someone who sounds like them or the guy next door.

Ed burps, eats, goes to the bathroom, and lets the audience know if it was a real dynamite dump!

Dre falls asleep, tells stupid stories, and fights like cats and dogs with our cohost, Lisa G.

We're real people like the everyday people you live with, work with, or meet every day. We're actual human beings and not those clone-drone jocks you find on the other end of the dial. Straight off-the-street flair. No nasal-type of voices, "This is Slammin' Ed and Jammin' Dre here at Power QVB . . ."

We're all about fun and entertainment. You don't have to know the rigid rules of radio to be good jocks. Just say how you really feel. So what if you offend someone?! People do it every day. We're paid to have fun and wake people up! We give it to them straight. Calvin Klein, so what? O.J., who cares? Gays this,

Blacks that, Puerto Ricans why? Everyone is fair game. We're equal-opportunity offenders. We're not fake during interviews. We ask the real questions the listeners want us to ask and as long as we're respectful, they'll answer or otherwise we give them the opportunity to say "no comment."

We say what we feel. We get calls sayin' we're disrespectful, but the truth is a hard pill to swallow. For instance, if a young girl calls in and says, "My baby's fatha don't take care of his kids." Ed will say, "How many kids do you have?" "Four." "When did he stop takin' care of them?" "After the first one!" Ed will go off, "Are you stupid! Why did you have three more??!" If we ask if she's stupid, we're not implying every single mother who has four kids is stupid. We're dealing with this individual, and the truth is the light, and if you don't like it, don't call in.

Our responsibility as role models is to tell the truth. You can't sugarcoat life, especially for kids, who happen to make up a good percentage of our listening audience. Show and tell them what's goin' on in the street. Educate them so no one else miseducates them. Equally expose the positive and the negative. There's a wonderful balance with our show. They know that we care because they hear us talk about violence, AIDS, Black men coming together, and lots of other positive stuff. They hear us ask the rappers why they say what they say, so they know we care. We have no power over programming, except half an hour each day when Dre plays his "Traffic Jam," a segment where he mixes all different kinds of music. Other than that we can't say, **"Yo, we're not going to play that record 'cause it promotes guns and violence."** So we have to educate our audience while this kind of music is being played.

Even though we seem to have great jobs, everyone has a little something to complain about when it comes to their job situation. No one's above that. The only people who don't complain about their bosses once in a while are people who work for themselves. It may seem like we work for ourselves, but we don't. Don't get us wrong: We have a lot of say when it comes to our morning show, and we're blessed to have the staff that we have to help us make it possible, but we still have to answer to the big bosses just like everyone else. We all sit around and say, "If I were the boss, I would run things this way, or I would do that differently." The one thing we can say when it comes to Hot 97 is that we want our

Ed, Dre, and Lisa.

coworkers to have the same opportunities we have at the station. We have an excellent manager that can negotiate for us, but a lot of our fellow coworkers aren't as fortunate. Don't get us wrong; we're not raking in the dough that way to say, "Give me a pay cut." Like just yesterday, Ed had no money. He had no money not because he didn't have cash, but in his pockets he had no loot. We're just like anybody else who works every day. Ed sat there and said, "Where the fuck am I going to get money from until my next check?" We're not ashamed to admit that cash doesn't always flow like we want it to, because we think the best of us do that, especially when we're trying to raise a family. Anyway, Ed thought—Ed actually sat and thought, and he sat in his bed and thought, "If all this shit ended tomorrow, who the fuck would take care of me? Not a goddamn soul but my mama. That's it. These muthafuckas in the street don't give a fuck about me." He's not talking about anybody close to him. Sometimes we think it's all about the power to control Ed and Dre.

Ed compares it to his brother's situation: "I talk to my brother a lot, and he has the same feelings about his job. He's a cop and the one thing that is foremost in his mind is the power to control what he does and his actions. Foremost the manipulation of his actions and the effect on the community. I think it's the same way for us. In no way do I think that our jobs are as important as my brother's, but I think the influence Dre and I have over our community is tremendous."

It's a heavy responsibility to uphold every day because we have to play both sides of the stick just like anybody else, but on a much bigger scale. That's a big reason why Lisa G cohosts the show with us. She brings a female voice and perspective that our audience needs to hear. She's an intelligent Jewish woman who brings her culture and her knowledge of the world as she knows it to the show. Who ever thought two Muslims and a Jew could ever run one of the nation's most successful morning shows? We all did!

It works for us, and we have a lot of fun at what we're doing. It's great to be part of a fresh new face in radio!

WHO'S THE MAN?

HOLLYWOOD COMES TO HARLEM:

Ed and Dre's Production Notebook

OUR first movie was a comedy called *Who's the Man?* It came out in spring '93 for New Line Cinema. If you knew what went on behind the scenes, it was more like a tragi-comedy.

We came up with the concept, then hired writer Seth Greenland to turn it into a screenplay. We wanted to shoot it in Harlem; you know, keep it real. We didn't know what real was 'til we found out what kind of budget New Line Cinema had in mind for us. Damn! Saying *Who's the Man?* had a low budget is like saying Kate Moss is slim.

There was fifty, sixty roles in the damn script, but no money to pay actors. So a whole lotta hip-hop talent got our backs and played all the parts for practically nothing. I don't know if New Line knew how large these "new" actors were, but they knew a bargain. We were proud that *Who's the Man?* had an almost total hip-hop cast. Rappers like Salt-n-Pepa, Ice-T, Naughty by Nature, Queen Latifah, Run-D.M.C., Heavy D, Cypress Hill, Flavor Flav, and Monie Love in the house, to name just a few. And the job they did was all that! We will always owe them—one and all—for being there.

I know what our fans're all thinking, Dre. You make a movie for Hollywood, you gotta be living large. Not true. See for yourself in this picture. Ice-T, Monie Love, and Freddie Foxxx, not even bitchin' an' all about how they had to freestyle on Amsterdam Avenue just so the extras could get to dress in the bathrooms at Mickey D's. That's troupers!

As the stars, it was only fair we got a little better dressing rooms than Mickey D's. But I'm telling you, not much! And I prefer not to discuss the plumbing, except to say that I've seen roomier accommodations in a Greyhound bus.

Mum's the word, Drizzay. I would never mention how we waited two hours on the set while you went home to get a better fit in your own king-sized porcelain throne room.

In this picture, I was assuring our fearless manager/producer, Charlie Stettler, that Ed wasn't gonna wander off to any more booty bars before the big chase scene. You see what lengths I go to for my man Ed?

Behind Dre and me are our dressing rooms. New Line thought we could share one, but when Dre pinned me behind the door on the first day, they backed off and got us each our own.

Our manager, Charlie Stettler, on location in Harlem. He was the producer of <u>Who's the Man?</u> One of his jobs was to harass New Line into doing the right thing. Check out the sumptuous spread they gave him for the Uptown Unit production office. A light and airy crib. Of course, on rainy days the ambiance was a little more moody . . .

Everybody's heard how films got a bad rep among women for having the director's casting couch. In our case, things was the other way around. This is our director, and <u>Yo! MTV Raps</u> partner-in-crime, Ted Demme, teaching a young actress how to do the Ed Lover Slap. For a honey to get a part in <u>Who's the Man?</u>, she had to master the technique and be prepared to wallop Ed in every scene. Making movies is not always all it's cracked up to be, right, Dre? Especially if you're Ed Lover.

Actually, Ed, those were my favorite scenes. Sometimes I'd promise the young lady dinner at the Plaza if she'd really give it all she had. I'm into Method acting.

Yo Yo doing her freestyle version of the Ed Lover Slap.

N Hollywood, Ed, it's always sunny. In New York, it rains a lot in November. It also sleets. It's gray and windy. Of course, you can keep dry under the awnings of the local bodegas. Then you get to warm up under the lights. Matter of fact, you fry your ass. But in the big league, the show must go on. And on. And on.

Dre, I don't get it. I know we only had thirty days to shoot that flick, but it seemed like we spent twenty-eight of them waiting!

This is us, waiting "five minutes" for our next scene. If I had a dollar for every time they told us to be ready on the set in five minutes, I'd have enough to make my own damn movie! Ed and I got a discount buying Intensive Care Lotion by the case. It works well for windburn or dehydration.

184

Photo from *Who's the Man*, copyright ©1993 New Line Productions, Inc. All rights reserved. Photo by Adger W. Cowans. Photo appears courtesy of New Line Productions, Inc.

I'm sorry, Ed, it's just another case of police brutality. Even if you are an African-American cop in Harlem, you don't stand a chance with Sergeant Denis on your case. This was not fair! I had to play the only cop in the world who wasn't allowed to eat doughnuts.

Quit bitchin', Dre. This was simply a case of art following life. Besides, your doughnuts were delicious. Especially the chocolate ones.

But Dre's right about one thing: Making a movie's a bitch! I don't think any of us ever worked harder. A lot of pressure. But even though everybody lived in each other's pocket, the whole crew ended up like a family. We all went crazy together. Especially Char-

Us and Charlie meeting with Kris Kross and Jermaine Dupri back in the Uptown production office. You can tell by the raggedy-ass shrub on the right. Dre and me were trying to sign up Kris Kross to be poster boys for our 1-800-ASS-WHIPPIN', but they wasn't having it. Nothin' personal. It was a career choice.

lie. We used to laugh every time he came on the set. It was like he had smoke comin' out of his ears. New Line was on his ass about the budget, Ted wanted mo' money, mo' time, wardrobe was running out of clothes, we loved the acting but bitched about the waiting, nobody liked the food, and everybody hated the weather. The last night of shooting was outdoors, and it snowed. And I had to get thrown through a window. I thought if that didn't kill me, I'd probably freeze to death.

A few days later, everybody's jumping and hollering, "It's a wrap!" Yeah, this time with a *w*. It was the hap-

A tender moment near the end of the shoot. The reason we're smiling is 'cause it was probably the only sunny day we had. Also, I think some New Line execs just left the set in disgust. It's times like that make the whole thing worthwhile. Hey, just kidding. But we sure felt good 'cause we knew we were almost finished shooting our first feature film.

piest time. Me and Dre sat down in my trailer and all of a sudden we both started to cry. We both knew we would have done anything if only our fathers could have been alive to share this moment with us.

But still, we were on top of the world. That's how much we knew, Ed, about making movies. The film might be in the can but we still had to be on the job. Next we had to loop (rerecord lost lines), then there was soundtrack meetings, marketing meetings, and the "P" word: promotion.

That was when we considered the idea that Charlie worked a plantation in another life. Up at five, cross-country—morning shows, talk shows, radio shows, lunches, malls, dinners, and nightclubs—every hour on the hour. Every day another city, but the hotels were all built by the same bad-taste guy. Yo, we're not complaining. Right, Charlie?

Who's the Man? opened as the #1 comedy in America that week. Siskel and Ebert gave us two thumbs up and said we were a great comedy team.

The premiere party at Roseland was the bomb. Thousands of people came to see our guests—Mary J. Blige, Jodeci, Naughty by Nature, and Cypress Hill—perform. MTV turned the whole party into a one-hour special that aired several times during our opening weekend.

We're really proud of what we did. We made a movie that was strong. We made people laugh. We made a lot of friends. And we did it on a shoestring. We did keep it real.

Can you believe it? After all that, we're still looking forward to our next movie. We have just one question, right, Doctor? Jim Carrey, what're you doing next year?

PICTURE CREDITS

WE'D LIKE TO EXTEND SPECIAL THANKS TO ALL
THE PEOPLE WHO HELPED MAKE THIS BOOK POSSIBLE:

The Roberts Family
The Brown Family
MTV Networks
Van Toffler
New Line Cinema
Robin Zlatin
Hot 97 WQHT-FM, New York
Donna Karan
Leslie Eric Francis
Patti Cohen
Larry Hotz
Jessica Kogan
Candace Sandy
The Management and Staff of WNYU, New York University Radio
Pamela McCullogh
Dave Goodson
Julia Cabrera
Jackie Bazan
Bonni Leon
Katy Riegel
Matt Shine
Theresa Horner
Eric Rayman
Steve Messina

NAKED
UNDER OUR CLOTHES

AVAILABLE ON ONE CASSETTE FROM
SIMON & SCHUSTER AUDIO

The hottest comedy team around, rap heavyweights Ed Lover and Doctor Dré are now on audio—totally free from the restraints of FCC regulations. Read by the authors in their own inimitable voices, NAKED UNDER OUR CLOTHES gives listeners off-the-wall humor, unforgettable pearls of wisdom, and uncensored thoughts on women, money, sex, fame and politics—more provocative than even their most devoted followers might expect!

NAKED UNDER OUR CLOTHES
Unzipped, Uncut and Totally Unplugged
Written and Read by Ed Lover and Doctor Dré
One Cassette/Approximate running time: 60 minutes
ISBN: 0-671-57386-1
Price: U. S. $9.95 Canada: $13.50

SIMON & SCHUSTER
AUDIO